Maine

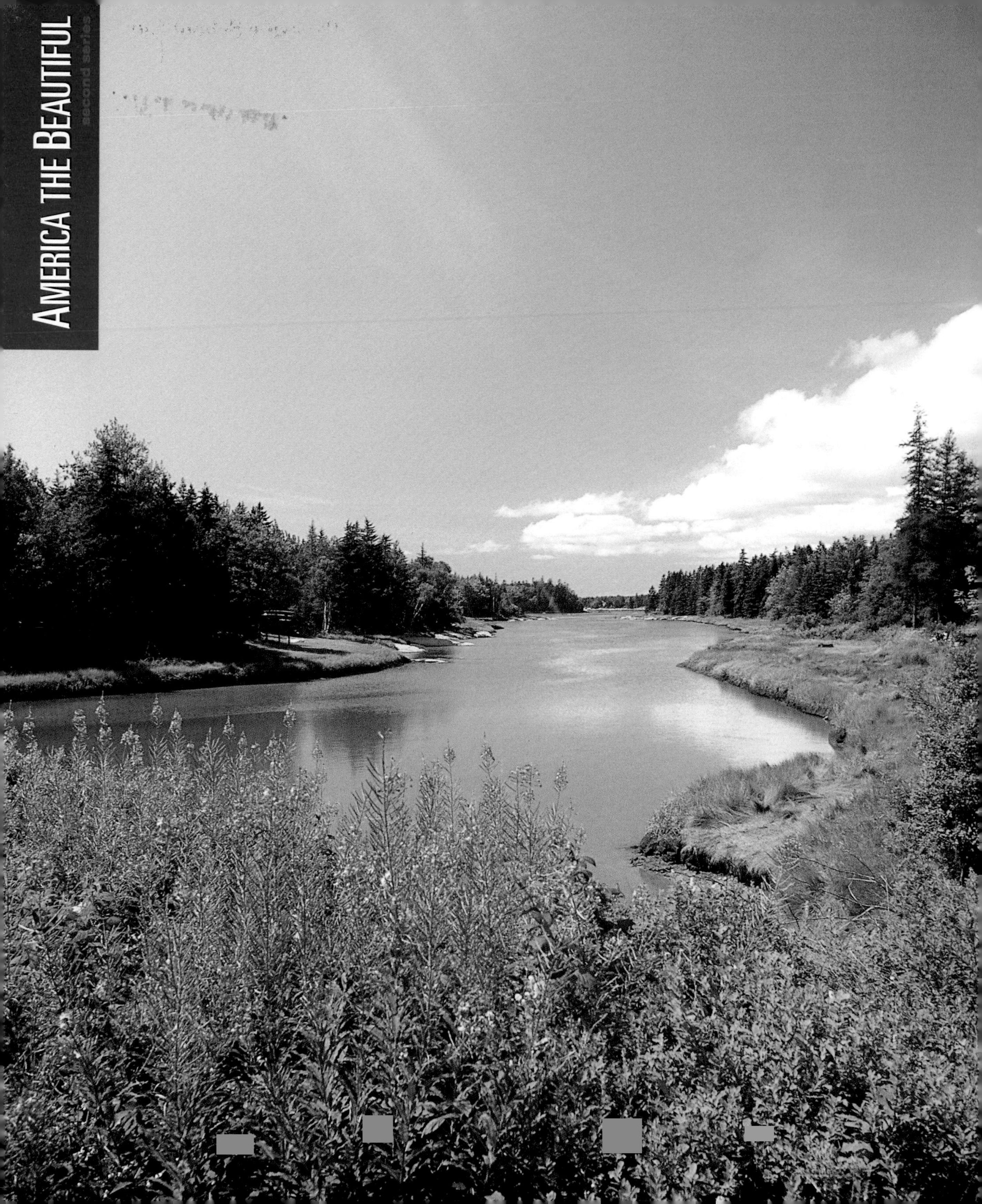
AMERICA THE BEAUTIFUL
second series

Maine

Deborah Kent

Children's Press®
A Division of Grolier Publishing
New York   London   Hong Kong   Sydney
Danbury, Connecticut

Frontispiece: One of Maine's beautiful lakes

Front cover: Portland Head Light, Cape Elizabeth

Back cover: Mount Katahdin

Consultant: Emily Herrick, Maine State Library

Please note: All statistics are as up-to-date as possible at the time of publication.

Visit Children's Press on the Internet at http://publishing.grolier.com

"Seascape," copyright © 1984 by May Sarton, from *Collected Poems 1930–1993* by May Sarton. Reprinted by permission of W. W. Norton & Company, Inc.

Book production by Editorial Directions, Inc.

Library of Congress Cataloging-in-Publication Data

Kent, Deborah.
    Maine / Deborah Kent.
      144 p. 24 cm. — (America the beautiful. Second series)
    Includes bibliographical references and index.
    Summary : Describes the geography, history, economy and industry, natural resources, arts and recreation, and people of the New England state of Maine.
    ISBN 0-516-20994-9
    1. Maine—Juvenile literature. [1. Maine.] I. Title. II. Series.
F19.3.K46   1999
974.1—dc21   98-33878
                                                              CIP
                                                              AC

GROLIER
PUBLISHING

Acknowledgments

I wish to extend my grateful acknowledgments to the Maine Tourism Information Service, the Maine State Historical Society, and the Portland Chamber of Commerce. Their generous assistance was invaluable to me in the writing of this book.

Harvesting potatoes

Logging

Lobstering

Robert E. Perry

Contents

Lobster trap floats

Bass Harbor Head lighthouse

Whale watching

Moose crossing sign

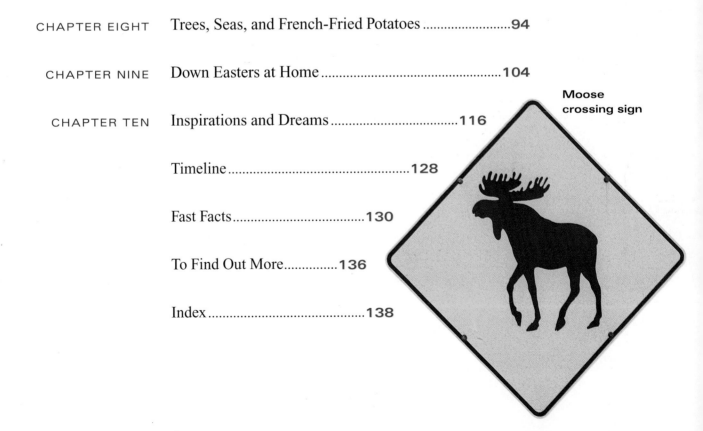

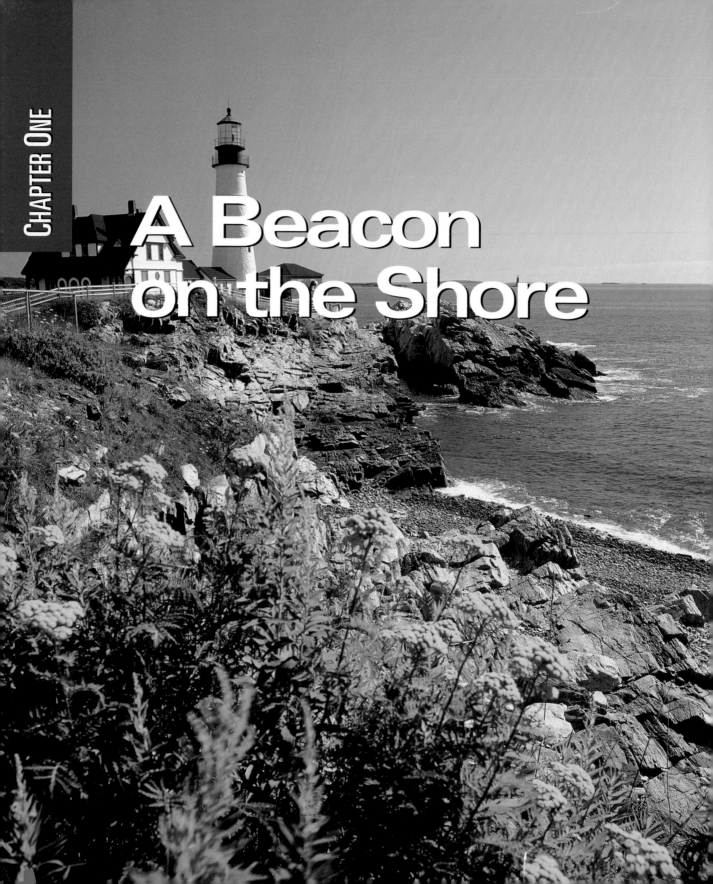

CHAPTER ONE

A Beacon on the Shore

Even if you have never set foot in the state of Maine, you have probably seen the Portland Head Light. In summer sun and winter gales, this famous lighthouse tower poses for visiting photographers. Its picture beams from magazines, guidebooks, and postcards, to say nothing of family albums. The lighthouse has even appeared in commercials for paint, toys, cosmetics, and breakfast cereal.

Rockport is one of Maine's charming coastal towns.

The Massachusetts legislature ordered construction of the Portland Head Light at Cape Elizabeth in 1791. At that time Maine was part of the state of Massachusetts. Its largest city, Portland, was one of New England's leading seaports. Ships needed a lighthouse to warn them of dangerous rocks as they sailed into Portland Harbor. For more than 200 years the Portland Head Light has served them well.

When outsiders think of Maine they usually picture its jagged, rock-strewn shore. They think of lobsters, fishing-boats, screaming gulls, and the tang of salt on the breeze. Indeed, Maine's coast is the most heavily populated part of the state. It is the hub of Maine's crucial fishing and tourist industries.

Yet the coast is only one dimension of this fascinating state. Maine has sparkling lakes and rivers with churning waterfalls. It has sprawling farms and charming small towns. It has factories that pour forth paper, furniture, and countless other products. Most of

Opposite: The Portland Head Light

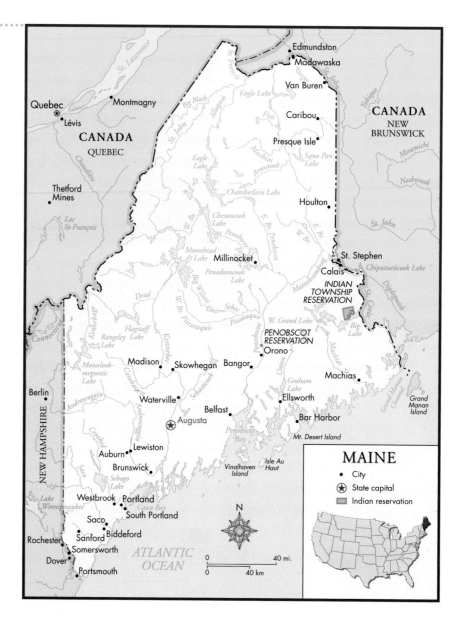

Map of Maine

MAINE
- • City
- ✪ State capital
- ▨ Indian reservation

0 ─── 40 mi.
0 ─── 40 km

N

all, Maine has trees—maple, birch, spruce, pine, and a host of others. At least 80 percent of the state is covered with forests. That's why it's often called the Pine Tree State.

Today, Mainers harvest timber from the woods and lobsters from the sea. But many would argue that Maine's greatest natural

resource is its stunning scenery. Millions of visitors flock to the state every year, drawn by its coves and beaches, lakes and hills. Like a gleaming lighthouse, Maine has always attracted people from near and far.

Maine is also known for stunning waterfalls, such as the Abol Falls on the Penobscot River.

CHAPTER TWO

Land of the Sunrise

Generations of farmers on Maine's Damaris-cotta Peninsula had a ready source of fertilizer for their fields. They used crushed oyster shells from a vast mound near the shore. The shell heap stretched for several hundred feet and was about 30 feet (9 m) high. Today, the remains of this shell mound are protected as a valuable archaeological site. The mound was created by some of Maine's earliest inhabitants. Like Mainers today, these ancient people harvested food from the sea.

Oyster-shell mounds left by early Native Americans along the shore of the Damariscotta River

Ochre and Arrows

Scientists believe that humans reached present-day Maine about 11,000 years ago. These people were the descendants of Asian tribes who crossed a narrow bridge of land that once connected Siberia with Alaska. Maine's first inhabitants were nomadic hunters. They followed herds of caribou and musk ox, creatures found only in the far north today. At that time, a great glacier was retreating from North America, and Maine was probably much colder than it is now.

About 4,000 years ago, a new group of nomads appeared in Maine. Archaeologists call them the Red Paint people. They often buried stone tools and weapons with their dead. These stone objects were painted with a reddish compound called ochre.

Opposite: The cliffs of Acadia National Park

Algonquin tribes lived in lodges throughout what is now Maine.

Over the centuries, new waves of migrants moved into Maine. They traveled in small bands, often loosely united into tribes. Tribes were usually governed by one or more chiefs and a council of advisors chosen by the people. Most of the tribes in Maine spoke Algonquin languages. Though these languages were all very different from one another, they were related through their grammar and word roots. Among the largest Algonquin tribes in Maine were the Penobscot and Passamaquoddy Indians.

The Native American peoples of Maine lived by hunting,

Messages in Stone

Maine's early hunters chipped spear points from a stone known as chert. Chert is easy to recognize because it has bright bands of blue and red. Deposits of chert are found in New York, Massachusetts, and Pennsylvania, but they do not occur in Maine. The use of chert suggests that these early Mainers traveled widely. To get chert they must have been trading with their southern neighbors. ■

fishing, and gathering nuts and berries. They also planted maize, or corn. During the winter, several families often lived together in a single longhouse covered with birch bark. A fire at each end of the longhouse provided the only heat. When the weather grew warmer the bands moved to fresh hunting grounds, camping in tents made of animal skins.

Warfare was a fact of life for the Indians of Maine. The tribes fought endlessly among themselves. But their most powerful enemies were the Iroquois, a united group of five tribes to the west. Sometime around the sixteenth century, several Algonquin tribes joined forces to resist the Iroquois. This league of Algonquin nations was known as the Abenaki or Wabanaki. The name *Abenaki* means "People of the Sunrise." The Abenaki took their name from the territory they lived in. Its capes and headlands jutted toward the east, as though they were reaching out for the rising sun.

Strangers from the Sea

In about the year A.D. 900, the Indians of Maine saw an awesome sight. A great ship with birdlike wings glided along the coast and came to rest in a rocky inlet. The men

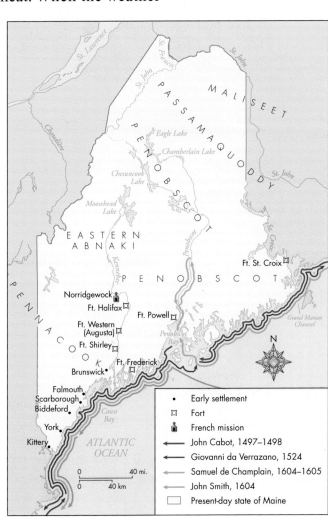

Exploration map of Maine

John and Sebastian Cabot are said to have traveled through Maine and as far south as the Carolinas.

who scrambled ashore had pale skin and yellow hair.

The newcomers were Norsemen from faraway Norway across the Atlantic Ocean. Historians believe that groups of Norse sailors landed frequently on the coast of Maine and eastern Canada over a period of about 300 years. They probably came to gather firewood and timber for the Norse colony on the treeless island of Greenland. Some evidence suggests that the Norsemen attempted to establish a colony on the Maine coast. However, their settlement did not survive for long. Probably it was destroyed by Indians or disease.

Nearly 500 years passed before Europeans again reached Maine's shores. Sailing under the English flag, John Cabot landed at Newfoundland, Canada. From there he sailed south along the

The Fabulous City

In 1568, a band of English pirates launched an ill-fated expedition against the Spaniards who had settled on the coast of Mexico. Somehow several members of the crew became separated from their fellows. Left behind on the Mexican shore, they headed north. After an extraordinary journey they reached Newfoundland, where they met a French ship that carried them home. One of these adventurers, David Ingram, published a lively but mildly embroidered account of his travels in the New World. Ingram's story described a splendid city called Norumbega, located somewhere on Penobscot Bay in present-day Maine. For decades afterward, Norumbega appeared on maps of North America. Not too surprisingly, however, no other explorer ever found the wondrous city of Norumbega. ■

Maine coast. Sebastian Cabot, John Cabot's son, claimed that he and his father sailed as far as the Carolinas. Many historians feel that Sebastian exaggerated his adventures, and his account is open to question.

In 1524, an Italian navigator named Giovanni da Verrazano steered along the coast, exploring some of Maine's bays and headlands. Da Verrazano sailed under the French flag and claimed the region for France, but the English were also taking an interest in the Maine coast. By 1600, English fishers had discovered vast schools of cod and other fish off Maine's shores.

In 1604, a band of French settlers under Samuel de Champlain established a colony on the St. Croix River. Today, the St. Croix marks the boundary between Maine and the Canadian province of New Brunswick. Champlain's colony survived for less than a year.

The French were not alone in their ambition to establish

Giovanni da Verrazano was one of the many European explorers to venture into Maine.

More Adventures of John Smith

Captain John Smith (1580?–1631) is usually associated with the English colony at Jamestown, Virginia. It was there that he had his famous meeting with Pocahontas, the Indian princess. But Captain Smith made several voyages of exploration up the North American coast. In 1604, three years before he landed in Virginia, he sailed along the shores of Maine to Casco Bay. When he tried to count the islands in the bay, Smith concluded that there were 365 of them, one for each day of the year. To this day, the islands in Casco Bay are called the Calendar Islands. Captain Smith's count was off, however; there are 122 islands rather than 365. ■

The Father of New France

Samuel de Champlain (1570?–1635) ran into bad luck when he tried to start a French colony on the St. Croix River. But, in 1608, he established a successful French settlement at Quebec in Canada. Under his leadership, Quebec became a French stronghold and a serious rival to English power in Maine. The scene was set for a long series of wars to determine which of the two European nations would control North America. ■

settlements in Maine. In 1607, a group of English colonists settled at the mouth of the Kennebec River. Known as Popham Plantation, the colony was named for its leader, Sir John Popham. The colonists were greeted by one of the harshest winters Maine could offer. Cold, hunger, and Indian attacks ravaged their ranks. After Popham fell ill and died, the colonists decided to abandon their settlement. The ships that brought them had long since sailed away, but fortunately, some of the surviving colonists had a knowledge of shipbuilding. They set to work and constructed a small sailing vessel that they named the *Virginia*. In the summer of 1608, they clambered aboard and sailed for England. The *Virginia* was the first ship ever built by Europeans on the eastern coast of North America.

The Europeans who visited Maine had failed to establish a lasting colony, but they learned that Maine was a land of rich natural resources. Its towering white pines made perfect masts for sailing ships. Dried and salted, its fish could feed hungry crews on long voyages. Best of all, its forests teemed with fox, mink, beaver, and other fur-bearing animals. Fur hats and capes were enormously

popular in Europe. In London and Paris, there were insatiable markets for pelts from Maine.

In the early 1600s, French and English fur traders explored the Maine woods. They bargained with the Indians, who were eager to exchange furs for muskets, iron kettles, and rum. But the traders exposed the Indians to a host of European diseases they had never encountered before. The Indians had no natural immunity to smallpox, diphtheria, or tuberculosis. Even measles proved to be a terrible scourge. Fearful epidemics wiped out whole villages. The once powerful Abenaki were sadly weakened and demoralized.

During the 1620s, several English settlements took root on the islands off the Maine coast. The name *Maine* may have come

The French and English traded with Maine's Native Americans for animal pelts.

The Absentee Landlord

Despite his Spanish-sounding name, Sir Ferdinando Gorges (1566–1647) was an English gentleman through and through. Gorges devoted most of his life to building the British colonies in New England. He had many friends in the English court, and he worked tirelessly to win their support for colonial ventures. Gorges wanted the colonies to be under the firm control of the Crown. He believed they would bring untold wealth and power to the mother country. Ironically, Gorges never saw the land of his dreams. He never set foot in North America. ◼

into use to distinguish the mainland from the islands offshore. The colonists struggled to clear the land and raise crops on the stony soil.

In 1622, King Charles I of England gave two of his supporters a large tract of land in present-day Maine and New Hampshire. These two land owners were John Mason and Sir Ferdinando Gorges. The tract was divided in 1629. Gorges received the northern portion—the largest share. His territory became the province of Maine. He established Maine's first colonial government in 1636, appointing officials to govern the settlers.

The colony grew steadily under Gorges, and later under his son Thomas. The colonists lived in scattered settlements on the islands and along the coast. As the years passed, settlements reached up the Kennebec and Penobscot Rivers. The town of Falmouth (today's Portland) developed a thriving shipbuilding industry. Other early settlements included Scarborough, Monhegan, Biddeford, and Waldoboro.

Farewell to the French

During the 1700s, England and France waged a series of wars over territory in the New World. The French won the support of the Algonquin Indians, while the British formed an alliance with the Iroquois.

The last of the French and Indian Wars, as this series of conflicts is called by today's historians, was fought from 1754 to 1763. France was defeated and forced to give up its claim to Maine forever. ■

Just south of Maine lay the prosperous English colony of Massachusetts. The Gorges family sold its holdings in Maine to Massachusetts in 1677. Maine would remain part of Massachusetts for the next 150 years.

The white pine was known for its thick trunk and was often used for building ships.

Fighting for Freedom

In 1691, Mainers heard an astounding piece of news. The Parliament in faraway London had declared that all white pine trees more than 24 inches (61 cm) in diameter belonged exclusively to the British Crown. Maine shipbuilders prized such trees because their thick, straight trunks were immensely valuable as ships' masts. Under the new law, these trees could provide masts only for the king's fleet. The shipbuilders were outraged. They felt that the new law infringed upon their freedom to conduct their business. The conflict over the white pines was an early sign of tension between Mainers and the British Crown.

After living in Maine for generations, the colonists knew it as their only home. They had less and less sense of connection with the mother country. But Great Britain saw Maine and its other colonies as a source of supplies and revenue. In the 1760s and early 1770s, Parliament imposed a series of new taxes on the colonists. It also passed an assortment of laws restricting imports and exports. Parliament's actions brought a storm of protest. In 1774, angry colonists from York, Maine, protested the new regulations by burning a cargo of tea from the British East India Company. This "York Tea Party" followed the famous Boston Tea Party of 1773.

On June 12, 1775, colonial forces captured the *Margaretta*, an armed British schooner, in Maine's Machias Bay. The capture of the *Margaretta* is regarded as the first naval encounter of the American

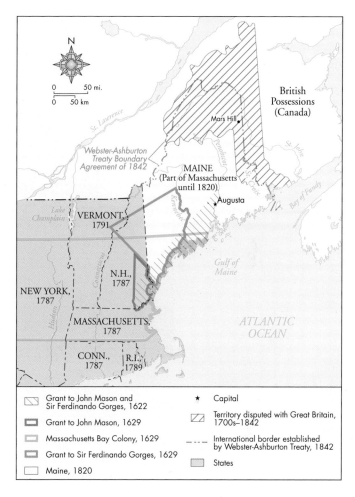

Historical map of Maine

Burnham Tavern

In 1775, colonists gathered in Burnham Tavern to plot the capture of the British schooner *Margaretta*. Built in 1770, the tavern still stands in Machias, Maine. A sign bears the original welcome: "Drink for the thirsty, food for the hungry, lodging for the weary, and good keeping for the horses." ■

Revolution (1775–1783). The British were incensed. They retaliated two months later by burning the port town of Falmouth.

During the American Revolution, Maine's loyalties were sharply divided. Many people fought fiercely for American independence. But others were staunch Loyalists, or Tories, who sided with the British. The town of Castine lay in a strong Loyalist area

at the mouth of the Penobscot River. When the British invaded Castine in 1779, they met little resistance.

It did not take long for news of Castine's fall to reach Massachusetts. Swiftly, Massachusetts launched a major naval force to recapture Castine. The Penobscot Expedition set out from Boston with forty heavily armed ships. But from the start nothing went according to plan. Several of the ships went down in a storm before they reached their destination. An outbreak of fever killed many of the expedition's men. Then the British got news of the intended attack in time to bring in reinforcements. The Penobscot Expedition suffered a terrible defeat. The survivors sank the last of their ships to keep them from falling into British hands.

The British may have done well in Maine, but in the end they lost the war. When the American Revolution was over, the thirteen colonies had knitted themselves into a new nation, the United States of America. Maine was still considered part of Massachusetts, but Mainers were eager to form a state of their own.

One of the American Revolution battles in Maine involved a brutal attack upon Falmouth, which is now the city of Portland.

An Ordinary Life

Martha Moore Ballard (1735–1812) was married at nineteen and gave birth to nine children, only six of whom lived to grow up. She worked as a midwife, delivering babies in and around Hallowell, Maine. For twenty-seven years, she faithfully kept a diary. Martha Ballard's diary gives us a rare view of a seemingly ordinary life in Maine just after the American Revolution.

On April 24, 1789, Martha Ballard described a particularly harrowing day of visits to deliver babies. Like most New Englanders of her time, she was careful to give God credit for bringing her safely through her many adventures. "A severe storm of rain. I was called at 1 hour P.M. from Mrs. Hussey's by Ebenezer Ewan. Crossed the [Kennebec] river in their boat. A great sea a-going. We got safe over, then set out for Mr. Ewan's. I crossed a stream on the way on fleeting logs and got safe over. Wonderful is the goodness of Providence! . . . Soon came to a stream. The bridge was gone. Mr. Ewan took the reins, waded through, and led the horse. Assisted by the same Almighty Power, I got safe through and arrived unhurt. Mrs. Ewan safe delivered at 10 hours evening of a daughter." ▪

President Thomas Jefferson's Embargo Act in 1807 had a negative impact on Maine merchants.

In 1807, President Thomas Jefferson tried to protect American manufacturers by banning foreign imports. Under Jefferson's Embargo Act, most trade with Europe was forbidden. Maine's merchants had earned their livelihood by trading with England, France, and other countries. For them, the Embargo Act proved disastrous. Grass grew on the docks of Portland, Kittery, and other port towns. Abandoned ships rotted in the harbors. The embargo was lifted in 1812, but long decades passed before Maine made a full recovery.

When Maine applied for statehood in 1819, the nation already had twenty-two states. Eleven of them allowed slavery within their borders, and eleven did not. Debate over the expansion of slavery was heating up in Congress. The slave-holding states wanted slavery to expand as new states joined the Union. Opponents of slavery hoped that it would be restricted as much as possible.

Few Mainers had ever owned slaves, and slavery was not permitted in Maine at all after the Revolution. If Maine entered the Union, it would join the ranks of the "free states."

Maine was admitted to the Union on March 15, 1820, under a plan called the Missouri Compromise. Maine entered as a free state and Missouri entered as a slave state. People on both sides of the slavery issue were temporarily appeased because the voting balance between slave and free states was maintained in the Senate.

Maine Becomes a State

In the early years of the United States, Maine was part of Massachusetts. The two were very different. Massachusetts had a fairly large, settled population. Its capital, Boston (below), was one of the most important cities in the United States. Maine, on the other hand, was thinly populated. Mainers felt that Massachusetts dominated their state government and believed they would have greater control of their affairs if Maine became a state. ■

CHAPTER THREE

The Vanishing Frontier

"Talk of mysteries! Think of our life in nature—daily to be shown matter, to come in contact with it—rocks, trees, wind on our cheeks! the solid earth! the actual world! Contact! Contact!"

—From *The Maine Woods*, by Henry David Thoreau, 1848

In the early 1800s, many Maine residents lived on farms, growing food for their own use and for sale in local markets.

Work for Many Hands

When Maine became a state in 1820, its population stood slightly below 300,000. Most people lived on the coast or along the lower reaches of the Kennebec and Penobscot Rivers. Families generally lived on small farms where they raised chickens, dairy cows, pigs, and a variety of fruits and vegetables. They grew most of their own food, though they might sell some eggs or fruit to markets in the towns.

Though farming was important, in a sense it was only part of the background. Maine was a state that faced the sea, and water

Opposite: A Maine forest

Down to the Sea in Ships

At the Maine Maritime Museum in Bath, visitors are treated to an unforgettable glimpse of Maine's shipbuilding industry. This open-air museum sprawls over 10 acres (4 ha) on the banks of the Kennebec River. The museum includes several fully restored boats that once cruised Maine's coastal waters. A unique program run by the museum offers eighteen-month apprenticeships in the arts of building, rigging, and restoring wooden boats. ■

provided Mainers with their essential livelihood. They fished, set lobster traps, and built boats and ships. Kittery, Thomaston, Portland (formerly Falmouth), and other ports turned out some of the finest sailing vessels in the world. Trading ships swept in and out of Maine's harbors. Strong deckhands unloaded crates of limes from Spain, sacks of sugar from the West Indies, and teakwood furniture from the Far East. Children from the coastal towns dreamed of "shipping out" to see the world. Boys as young as fourteen signed aboard trading schooners and left their homes

A sawmill on the Penobscot River in the 1850s

behind. They might be gone for two or three years at a time. Life at sea was filled with perils. Many sailors never returned at all.

While men took to the sea, most women kept busy at home. They tended the cows and chickens and cared for the children. They sewed most of the family's clothing. Often they grew deeply lonely.

Sometimes a group of women gathered to stitch together a patchwork quilt. Such quilting parties were a welcome break in the daily routine of hard work. They gave the women a chance to exchange news and enjoy some precious moments of laughter and good company.

When textile mills opened in Lewiston and Auburn, girls began to work outside the home as their brothers did. Some mills provided dormitories for their workers, who were mainly young women in

The First Environmentalist

Henry David Thoreau (1817–1862) was born and raised in Massachusetts. As a young man, he grew disenchanted with city life. He fled civilization to live in the woods at Walden Pond near the Massachusetts town of Concord. Thoreau questioned the values of the growing nation and lamented the destruction of the wilderness. During his lifetime, most people thought the frontier was inexhaustible, and hailed progress as a God-given virtue. People dismissed Thoreau as an eccentric and his message was mocked and ignored. Today, Thoreau is recognized as a pioneer in the movement to preserve our natural environment.

Beginning in 1838, Thoreau made three trips to northern Maine. He traveled its rivers by canoe with a Penobscot Indian guide. Thoreau was thrilled by the state's wildness, though deeply troubled by the increasing ravages of the logging industry. His cherished memories of Maine stayed with him until the end of his life. It is said that Thoreau's dying word was, "Moose!" ■

their teens and twenties. There was nothing romantic about work in the mills. Mill hands labored twelve- and fourteen-hour days, hurrying back and forth to operate noisy mechanical looms. Maine's first mills opened in 1819. By the 1840s, the state was a leading textile producer.

With its vast stretches of untouched forest, Maine was the last frontier on the East Coast of the United States. Eager to exploit this untamed land, people poured in from the more settled regions of Massachusetts and New Hampshire. They felled trees, uprooted stumps, and carved new farms out of the wilderness.

The shipbuilding industry took a major toll on Maine's forests.

For two centuries, woodsmen had cut down the tallest and straightest white pines to make into towering ship's masts. White pine disappeared from the coast, then from farther inland. As the supply dwindled, loggers turned to other trees that could serve other purposes. They cut spruce, hemlock, and hardwoods such as maple and oak. Sawmills turned logs into planks for houses and furniture. More and more axes rang out, more great trees fell, and the wilderness steadily retreated.

General Winfield Scott is credited for settling a border dispute between Canada and Maine in 1839.

Calls to Arms

As Mainers pushed northward into the wilderness, they frequently encountered settlers from Canada. Sometimes these meetings led to arguments and fistfights. The two nations were in sharp disagreement about Maine's northern boundary. Maine claimed all of the land north to the St. Lawrence River. Canada insisted that its territory reached south to the town of Mars Hill.

After a series of violent skirmishes, Mainers prepared for war. In 1839 the state rallied a militia force of more than 3,000 men. Word reached the militia that troops from the Canadian province of New Brunswick planned to attack. Armed for battle, the Maine militia marched 200 miles (322 km) northward through the snow. U.S. general Winfield Scott avoided

Closing the Taverns

In 1815, a group of Mainers gathered in Portland to form the state's first "total abstinence society." The society's goal was to end the drinking of alcoholic beverages in the state. Maine became the first state to forbid the sale and manufacture of alcoholic beverages, passing a strong temperance law in 1851. The law excited much controversy, and underwent a series of changes over the years. Nevertheless, Maine remained a "dry" state until 1934. ■

bloodshed by working out a diplomatic solution to the conflict. For the next three years, both nations occupied the contested territory. The Aroostook War, as the conflict is known, was finally settled by the Webster-Ashburton Treaty of 1842. Under the treaty, Maine gave up its claim to about 5,500 square miles (14,245 sq km) of land.

Most Mainers believed that slavery was an evil that ran against the teachings of the Bible. Some sided with the abolitionists, people who wanted to abolish slavery completely. But not all Mainers took an antislavery stand. Many merchants in the coastal towns profited from the slave trade and feared they would lose money if slavery were outlawed. Though they did not own slaves themselves, they imported cotton, sugar, and other goods that were produced with slave labor.

As tension over the slavery question mounted across the nation, the antislavery faction in Maine gathered momentum. Eventually Maine took a strong antislavery position.

In 1861, shots were fired at Fort Sumter in South Carolina, and the United States plunged into a bloody civil war. Mainers rushed forward to defend the Union. Some 73,000 Mainers served in the American Civil War. One in every ten soldiers died, either in battle or of smallpox and other diseases that swept the camps.

A Foe of Slavery

Hannibal Hamlin (1809–1891) of Paris, Maine, was a dedicated fighter for the abolition of slavery. Hamlin went to Congress in 1843 and served in the U.S. Senate from 1848 to 1856. In 1857, Hamlin was elected as governor, but he left his post the same year to go back to the senate. In 1860, the Republican candidate for president, Abraham Lincoln, chose Hamlin to be his running mate. During Lincoln's first term in the White House, Hamlin pushed for the emancipation, or freeing, of the slaves. When he ran for president again in 1864, Lincoln hoped that the Civil War (1861–1865) would soon be over. He looked toward reconciliation with a defeated South, and selected Andrew Johnson of Tennessee to run for vice president. Hamlin returned to the U.S. Senate (1869–1881), where he worked to secure equal rights for African-Americans in the Southern states. ■

The Professor Who Went to War

In 1862, Joshua L. Chamberlain (1828–1914) left his teaching post at Bowdoin College and joined the Union army as a lieutenant colonel. Chamberlain had no formal training in the art of war, but he was a devoted student of military history. According to legend, he studied military textbooks on the long train ride from Maine to Washington, D.C., where he accepted his commission. Chamberlain was soon promoted to the rank of general. He served with distinction at the Battle of Gettysburg, where he won praise for his ability to take decisive action. On April 9, 1865, General Chamberlain had the honor of accepting the Confederate surrender at Appomattox Court House in Virginia. After the war, Chamberlain went back to Bowdoin College and once again lived the quiet life of a professor. ▪

Moving Forward, Holding Back

The wooden ships Maine made famous soon gave way to steamships made of iron and steel.

Shipbuilding was a cornerstone of Maine's economy from the day the first colonists built the *Virginia*. For more than 200 years, Maine's shipyards turned out sleek, handsome wooden sailing vessels. But after the Civil War, the demand for wooden ships declined steeply. The world was in love with speed and progress. Steamships made of iron and steel were faster and more efficient than the vessels of the past.

As the market for wooden ships collapsed, many Maine shipyards shut down. But some shipbuilders made the crucial transition from wood to iron and steel. During the 1880s, shipyards in Bath began to pro-

The Plumed Knight

In the years after the Civil War, the most prominent politician from Maine was James G. Blaine (1830–1893). Born in Pennsylvania, Blaine moved to Augusta in 1854 to edit a Republican newspaper, the Kennebec *Journal*. His work put him in contact with many Republican leaders and launched his political career. Blaine was an eloquent speaker and a major Republican figure in Washington from 1869 until 1892. Though his career was tarnished by scandals, his supporters saw him as a fierce fighter for noble causes. They nicknamed Blaine "the Plumed Knight."

Blaine served in the U.S. Senate and sought the Republican nomination for president in 1880 and 1892. He was appointed secretary of state by two presidents, James A. Garfield and Benjamin Harrison. In this position he worked to establish a Pan-American Conference to ensure peace in the Western Hemisphere. His efforts were largely unsuccessful, but he was ahead of his time in recognizing the importance of U.S. relations with Latin America. ■

duce steam-powered vessels. The new ships were not graceful, but they moved cargo more quickly than ever before. Shipbuilding remained one of Maine's most important industries.

The logging industry also underwent dramatic changes in the late nineteenth century. Timber was no longer in demand at the

The Maine forests supplied a rich logging industry.

shipyards, but more and more people were learning to read and write, and the nation was hungry for paper. Wood from Maine's forests was ground into pulp at newly opened paper mills. Waterfalls on the state's rivers generated power to keep the mills running. The growth of the paper industry made logging more important than ever.

In the 1840s, an artist named Thomas Cole visited the Maine coast. Cole spent several summers painting rocky cliffs, gulls, and fishing boats. His pictures celebrated a quiet, simple way of life that was already vanishing in other parts of the country.

Cole's work lured dozens of other painters to Maine. After the Civil War, wealthy families from Boston and New York followed the artists. They packed up their entire households, complete with

Cottages by the Sea

The rusticators of the 1880s and 1890s came from the richest Boston families. They wanted the simple life, but they wanted to enjoy it in luxury. Many of their "cottages" were actually mansions. They had marble fireplaces, sweeping mahogany stairways, and libraries stocked from floor to ceiling with leather-bound books. One such cottage in Bar Harbor had twenty-eight bathrooms. ■

servants and furniture, and headed to Maine for the summer. These "rusticators," as they were called, sought an escape from the noise and bustle of the cities. They were enchanted by Maine's quaintness and rural ways. Like Thoreau, they were thrilled by the sight of the deer and the moose. In the woods and villages of Maine, they found something that much of the nation had already lost. Yet even in Maine this natural serenity was beginning to disappear, as it made its way into the twentieth century.

CHAPTER FOUR

Building a Future

n 1909, workers at the Bath Ironworks on the Kennebec River began a gargantuan task. They started construction of the 329-foot (100-m) battleship *Wyoming*. The *Wyoming* was the biggest ship ever built in a U.S. shipyard up to that time. It launched Maine into a new century of change and achievement.

Over There!

Bands played and flags unfurled in 1917 as the United States entered World War I (1914–1918). Young men marched to a popular song that declared, "We won't be back till it's over over there!" Like the rest of the nation, Maine was swept along by the patriotic tide. Towns competed to see which one could send the most volunteers to the fighting front. More than 35,000 young men from Maine served in the armed forces. The majority of them were farm boys who had rarely left their hometowns before. Suddenly, they found themselves in the midst of combat on the faraway fields of Germany and France.

When World War I was over, the returning soldiers brought back startling new ideas. They were no longer content to get up each morning to plow stony fields or set out each day in fishing boats. They talked with excitement about big cities, easy money, and progress.

The Bath Ironworks built some of the United States' finest battleships.

Opposite: Lobster trap floats at Bass Harbor

Journeys North

The Arctic Museum in Brunswick, Maine, pays unique tribute to the arctic explorer Robert E. Peary (1856–1920). Peary was a graduate of Maine's Bowdoin College. Beginning in 1891, he led a series of daring expeditions across the frozen reaches of Canada and Greenland. Many historians believe that Peary was the first person of European heritage to reach the North Pole, on his 1909 expedition. Peary's wife Josephine accompanied him on this trip. Their daughter Marie Ahnighito Peary was the first white child born north of the Arctic Circle. Little Marie was hailed in the press as "The Snow Baby."

Visitors to the Arctic Museum can see stuffed polar bears, ivory carvings made by the Inuit people (once called Eskimos), and other memorabilia from the far north. The museum also has Peary's original journals. ■

Many returning veterans did not stay in Maine for long. They moved on to Boston, New York, and other cities, hoping to make their fortunes. Those who did stay worked to make Maine more up to date. Soon, power and telephone lines fanned out across the state. Rural homes got running water for the first time. A radio station began to broadcast music and news from Bangor. Once-isolated farms and villages were connected to the rest of the world.

As early as the 1840s, potatoes were among Maine's most important crops. During the 1920s, potato farming became big business in the state. Aroostook County in the far north rose as Maine's potato capital. The most successful farmers bought more and more land. Then in the 1930s, the United States fell into a terrible economic depression. The people of Maine were hit hard. Farm prices tumbled, shipyards shut down, and thousands of people could not find work. By tradition, Mainers were fiercely self-

Prohibition is a Howling Success in Maine

Rum-Running and Bathtub Gin

In 1920, an amendment to the U.S. Constitution forbade the manufacture or sale of alcoholic beverages anywhere in the country. Though the state of Maine had passed similar "prohibition laws" dating back to 1851, enforcement of these laws had never been easy and many farmers added to their income by making and selling illegal homemade whiskey. The enforcement problems multiplied when Prohibition went nationwide. Countless backwoods families in Maine made whiskey at home to sell on the black market. Smugglers hid boatloads of spirits in coves along the lonely Maine coast. Unfamiliar with the rugged shore, federal officials could do little to stop this illegal traffic. Maine finally repealed its Prohibition laws in 1934, a year after the federal ban on alcohol was lifted. ■

Potato farming was an important business for Maine in the 1920s.

reliant. They believed in tackling their own problems without getting anyone's help. Now many families could not put food on their tables without the aid of government programs. Mainers were deeply pained at accepting "federal handouts," but, faced with starvation, they had no choice.

In War and Peace

The United States entered World War II (1939–1945) on December 7, 1941, after Japanese bombers attacked the U.S. naval base at Pearl Harbor in Hawaii. Stunned and outraged, the United States hurled itself full force into the war effort. Once more,

Rebuilding the Fleet

During World War II, shipyards in Maine made an extraordinary contribution to American naval forces. The New England Shipbuilding Company in South Portland produced hundreds of cargo vessels called Liberty ships. More than seventy submarines were launched from the Kittery Naval Yard. The Bath Ironworks manufactured about one-fourth of all the destroyers used during World War II. Because so many men were away fighting, a large percentage of the workers in these shipyards were women. ■

Maine citizens put on uniforms. Shipyards reopened, running on three shifts a day. Men and women in Portland, Kittery, and Bath worked feverishly to help rebuild the United States' naval power.

The war stimulated Maine's economy in many ways. Textile factories turned out crisp new uniforms and shoe factories made heavy-duty army boots. Businesses in Portland rushed to serve the thousands of sailors stationed at Casco Bay Naval Base.

Maine's economy remained relatively strong even after

Maine shipyards were vital during World War II and through the 1960s.

World War II ended in 1945. Shipyards continued to be busy through the 1960s. Improvements in shipping and food preservation helped farmers sell their produce to new, far-flung markets. With the increased use of chemical fertilizers and pesticides, farmers got higher yields from each acre of land.

In the wake of the war, the nation experienced a dramatic building boom. As housing developments sprang up across the country, Maine's timber industry flourished. Huge tracts of forest were cut down to provide wood for new homes. Maine's paper industry, too, saw a tremendous upsurge. At the same time, Maine's long-standing textile and leather industries held firm.

In the 1960s, however, the picture took on more somber tones. New England factory owners grumbled that workers were demanding exorbitant wages. They looked for a workforce that would accept a lower pay scale. Some plants shifted their operations to the Carolinas and other southern states, and some moved to the teeming cities of Asia. By the 1980s, most of Maine's textile and shoe factories had shut their doors. Also, the growing number of large, highly mechanized farming operations drove most small family-run farms out of business.

To combat rising unemployment, Maine tried to lure new businesses into the state. The legislature passed laws giving tax breaks to corporations. An ambitious highway-construction program made transportation more efficient for businesses and for the general public.

During the 1980s and 1990s, Maine paid special attention to an industry that had taken root nearly a century before. It made a major commitment to the development of tourism.

In 1972, the Penobscot and Passamaquoddy Indians brought a major lawsuit against the state of Maine. The tribes charged that Congress had never ratified a 1794 treaty by which Maine (as part of Massachusetts) seized much of the Indians' ancestral land. The Native Americans now demanded the return of some 12.5 million acres (5.1 million ha)—about two-thirds of the state. After years in court, the Indians won their case in 1980. The state did not give them the land they demanded, but it agreed to pay them $81.5 million. The Indians used most of the money to set up a fund to buy 300,000 acres (121,500 ha) of prime timberland. ■

Working with the Land

License plates on automobiles in Maine proudly bear one of the state's nicknames—Vacationland. Especially in the last two decades of the twentieth century, Maine transformed its woods and beaches into a visitors' paradise. Hotels and rental cabins mushroomed along shores where once only the wealthy could afford to spend their summers. State fisheries stocked lakes and streams with trout, bass, and landlocked salmon to entice sports fishers. Hunting lodges opened in the once-remote backwoods. Ski lifts operated on Maine's mountains, and snowmobile trails snaked through the forests.

The Hotel Pemaquid is just one example of the many hotels available for vacationers.

By the 1990s, logging became a problem in Maine as thousands of acres of trees were destroyed.

Tourists flocked to Maine, entranced by its wildness and beauty. But visitors were often dismayed to hear the roar of chainsaws as they set up their rustic campsites. By the 1990s, giant logging companies owned most of the state's undeveloped land. In the nineteenth century, loggers cut only the largest and most valuable trees, leaving the rest to grow for another time. However, twentieth-century logging companies found it cheaper and easier to clear-cut. Their power saws cut down thousands of acres of trees, leaving huge scars on the once lavish land. After viewing the timberland from the air, writer John McPhee stated, "Much of northern Maine now looks like an old and badly-tanned pelt, the hairs coming out in tufts."

In the 1980s and 1990s, environmentalists fought to preserve portions of Maine's forest as state and national parkland, but the big logging and paper companies had tremendous power in the state legislature. Environmental measures often went down to defeat.

The fishing industry, too, was a source of controversy as the twentieth century drew to a close. Overfishing and pollution caused a sharp drop in the numbers of cod and other ocean fish

John D. Rockefeller, Conservationist

One wealthy vacationer who fell in love with Maine early in the twentieth century was millionaire John D. Rockefeller (1874–1960). Rockefeller realized that development threatened to destroy much of Maine's natural beauty. In 1919, he purchased 11,000 acres (4,455 ha) of land on Mount Desert Island. He gave this property to the world by helping to create Acadia National Park.

Rockefeller made millions of dollars in the oil business, but he determined to keep cars out of his new park as much as possible. He laid out 57 miles (92 km) of "carriage roads" to be reserved for horse-drawn vehicles. Today, these trails are a delight to cyclists, joggers, horseback riders, and hikers—and cars are still forbidden. ■

in Maine's waters. Some scientists warned that Maine's lobster supply might meet a similar fate. Environmentalists pushed for catch limits, arguing that the lobster population needed time to renew itself. But people in the lobster industry pointed out that they were hauling in bigger catches than ever. The proposed laws would force them to harvest fewer lobsters, and would allow them to keep only the largest lobsters they trapped. If these rules went into effect, many of these fishers feared they would be put out of business.

Unlike most other states on the East Coast, Maine remains largely rural. The land and sea are still its greatest resources. How it chooses to use its natural wealth will determine the state's future.

Maine's commercial fishing became controversial as fish populations declined and pollution increased.

CHAPTER FIVE

Forests, Lakes, and Shores

n endless variations on a theme
    The waves come in and lace the rocky shore.
One after one long ripples rise and spread
Until they break in necklaces of foam
Or fountain up in spume, an endless store—
The gentle sea is singing in my head.
        —"Seascape," from *Letters from Maine*, by May Sarton

Camden is one of Maine's most picturesque villages.

Along the Coast

Maine perches at the far northeastern corner of the United States. It is one of the six states in the region known as New England. On the southwest, Maine borders New Hampshire. To the north, it

Down East to Maine

In the days of sailing ships, few things mattered more than the direction of the wind. Captains who sailed from Boston knew that the breezes would carry them eastward to the Maine coast.

Because Maine lay downwind from Boston, it was said to be "down east." To this day, Maine is often called the "Down East State," though not many people remember why. ■

**Opposite:
Moosehead Lake**

To the Lighthouse

With its jagged, rocky coast, Maine can be treacherous for sailors. In the nineteenth century, Mainers built a string of lighthouses to help ships navigate safely. Each tower was staffed by a keeper who made sure the light was always burning brightly. Today, electric lighting has made the lighthouse keeper's job obsolete. But some sixty lighthouses still stand guard along Maine's shores, including Bass Harbor Head

(photo), reminders of the state's rich maritime history.

Saddleback Lodge Light Station is a 42-foot (13-m) tower perched on a barren island between Vinalhaven and Isle au Haut. Lonely lighthouse keepers used to bring sacks of soil to the island in an effort to plant gardens on the rocky ground. Their flowers and vegetables were always washed away with the first storm.

The Stockton Springs Lighthouse stands at the mouth of Penobscot Bay. A bell in its 31-foot (9-m) wooden tower used to toll in stormy weather. The bell, having been replaced by a booming foghorn, is now on display at the foot of the tower. The lighthouse on Monhegan Island is a gray, cone-shaped tower. The keeper's house has been converted into a small museum with information on the history of the island. ◼

thrusts like a jabbing thumb between the Canadian provinces of Quebec and New Brunswick.

Spreading over 33,741 square miles (87,389 sq km), Maine ranks thirty-ninth in size among the fifty states. It is by far the largest state in the New England region. Maine could hold all of the other New England states snugly within its borders. Despite its size,

Bar Harbor, one of Maine's many resorts

however, Maine is thinly populated. About 80 percent of the state is still covered with forests.

Most Mainers are never far from the sound of the sea. The majority of the population lives in the Coastal Lowlands, a narrow strip of land reaching about 20 miles (32 km) inland along the Atlantic shore. On the map, Maine's coast looks jagged, like a comb with broken and twisted teeth. From Kittery to the New Brunswick border, Maine has 228 miles (367 km) of coastline. But if you include the hundreds of inlets, coves, islands, and capes, the coast would actually measure about 3,500 miles (5,632 km).

Maine's coast is dotted with islands. Many are little more than mossy rocks jutting above the waves, while others are big enough to support towns and forests. The largest is Mount Desert Island,

Cadillac Mountain, the highest peak on the Atlantic seaboard of the United States, soars 1,550 feet (467 m) above sea level on Mount Desert Island. It seems to rise straight out of the ocean. Another extra-ordinary feature on Mount Desert Island is a deep cavern called the Thunder Hole. Seawater rushes into the cavern, swirls around, and bursts out with a roar like crashing thunder. ■

home of Acadia National Park. The town of Bar Harbor on the island's eastern tip is now a thriving summer resort. Other islands include Deer Isle, Isle au Haut, and Vinalhaven. Like Mount Desert Island, they have active summer communities.

Into the North Woods

Away from the coast, the land rises in a series of hills and plateaus. The White Mountains zigzag through northern and western Maine. These steep, rugged peaks are an extension of the Appalachian Range that stretches all the way to northern Alabama. Maine has

Hiking the Trail

Many serious backpackers dream of some day hiking the length of the Appalachian National Scenic Trail. The Appalachian Trail, as it is commonly called, winds for 2,000 miles (3,200 km) across fourteen states through some of the most beautiful country in eastern North America. The trail begins near the foot of Mount Katahdin in northern Maine and ends at Springer Mountain in Georgia. Experienced hikers claim that the Maine segment of the trail is especially challenging because of its steep climbs and tangled woods. ■

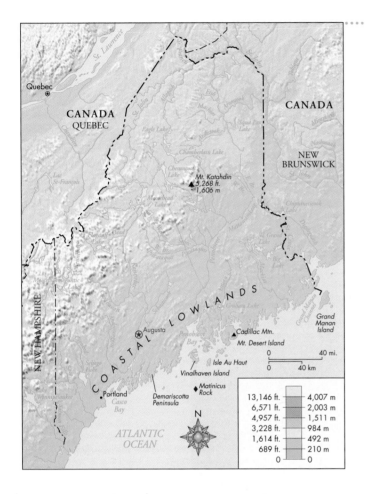

Maine's topography

nine mountains that are more than 4,000 feet (1,219 m) high. The tallest peak in the state is Mount Katahdin, at 5,268 feet (1,606 m) above sea level. The peak is often shrouded in fog. After writer Henry David Thoreau climbed Katahdin in 1846 he wrote, "It was like sitting in a chimney and waiting for the smoke to blow away. It was in fact a cloud factory."

Nestled among Maine's hills and mountains are some 2,500 natural lakes and ponds. The largest of these is Moosehead Lake, 35 miles (56 km) long and covering 117 square miles (303 sq km). Fly-in Lake is the only natural habitat of the square-tail trout, coveted by sports fishers. Other lakes include Chamberlain, Sebago, West Grand Lake, and Big Lake.

Maine's rivers once served as highways for Abenaki Indians who paddled birch-bark canoes. Later, the rivers carried white pine logs to shipyards on the coast. Today, the same rivers generate hydroelectric power. The most important rivers in the state are the Kennebec, the Penobscot, and the Androscoggin. The St. John River flows north from Maine into Quebec. The St. Francis and St. Croix Rivers help form the border between Maine and Canada.

The northern half of Maine, a vast area the size of Vermont and New Hampshire combined, is almost entirely covered with

Forever Wild

In 1930, Maine's former governor Percival Baxter set aside 200,000 acres (81,000 ha) of forest in northern Maine as Baxter State Park. The governor pledged that this land would remain "forever wild." Today, no paved roads penetrate the park, and there are no utility hookups for recreational vehicles. The park is so popular that campgrounds are often booked months in advance. Baxter State Park is the largest wilderness park in Maine. ▧

forests. Nearly all of this land belongs to giant timber and paper companies that harvest the trees as a cash crop. Loggers leave a narrow buffer zone of trees around most lakes and along rivers and streams. These bands of untouched woodland make the state

Drivers often encounter moose on Maine roads.

The mink is just one of the many creatures that live in the Maine woods.

more attractive to visitors and provide a habitat for many of Maine's birds and animals.

Wild Maine

"A moose started to cross the road in front of us. [My friend] Bill doesn't have a bumper sticker saying 'I brake for moose!' but he braked anyway. Most Mainers take it for granted that any critter over half a ton has the right of way." As biologist Bernd Heinrich suggests in this lighthearted account, meetings between moose and Mainers are not uncommon. Highways in northern Maine are marked with yellow Moose Crossing signs. More than 20,000 of these massive animals are thought to live in the state.

The Maine woods are home to dozens of creatures large and small. Black bears and bobcats still survive in remote areas of the far north. Beavers, mink, otters, and muskrats live in lakes and streams. The fisher, a rare member of the weasel family, hunts on the ground and in the treetops. It is the only carnivore that will attack and devour the prickly porcupine. White-tailed deer, raccoons, skunks, opossums, and red and gray squirrels are found throughout the state.

Birds, too, abound in Maine. The state is the nesting ground for twenty species of warblers. The flutelike notes of the hermit thrush enrich

Maine's Geographical Features

Total area; rank	33,741 sq. mi. (87,389 sq km); 39th
Land; rank	30,865 sq. mi. (79,940 sq km); 39th
Water; rank	2,878 sq. mi. (7,448 sq km); 13th
***Inland water;* rank**	2,263 sq. mi. (5,861 sq km); 9th
***Coastal water;* rank**	613 sq. mi. (1,588 sq km); 9th
Geographic center	Piscataquis, north of Dover
Highest point	Mount Katahdin, 5,268 feet (1,606 m)
Lowest point	Sea level along the coast
Largest city	Portland
Population; rank	1,233,223 (1990 census); 38th
Record high temperature	105°F (41°C) at North Bridgton on July 10, 1911
Record low temperature	–48°F (–44°C) at Van Buren on January 19, 1925
Average July temperature	67°F (19°C)
Average January temperature	15°F (–9°C)
Average annual precipitation	41 inches (104 cm)

Matinicus Isle

Some 20 miles (32 km) beyond the mouth of Penobscot Bay a craggy island juts from the sea. It has no human inhabitants, but during the spring and summer it is always noisy and crowded. Matinicus Isle is the only North American nesting site of a shorebird called the common puffin. Thousands of these birds gather here each year, calling to each other in loud, raucous squawks. Tour boats visit the island regularly from Boothbay Harbor, allowing visitors to see this lively colony at close range. ■

The sugar maple is one of Maine's hardwood trees.

summer evenings, and the joyful outpouring of the winter wren is a delight to hikers in the deep woods. The eerie cry of the common loon floats across many lakes and ponds. Other waterbirds include several species of ducks and herons.

Maine's northern forests are lush with evergreens: white and red pine, hemlock, spruce, and eastern balsam. Hardwood trees include white birch, beech, ash, white oak, and sugar maple. Wild blueberries flourish in Maine's wetlands. Among Maine's wild-flowers are forty-five species of orchids. These delicate plants

Sugaring Time

Long ago, Maine's Native Americans learned to harvest sweet sap from the sugar maple. Mainers continue the practice today by boring holes into tree trunks and catching the dripping sap in buckets. Through a long process of boiling and straining, this raw sap is transformed into maple sugar. Maple sugar is used in making delicious candies, ice cream toppings, and pancake syrup. ■

The Scourge of the North Woods

Every spring, Mainers brace themselves for the coming of the black flies. These tiny insects descend in bloodthirsty swarms each June. Their relentless stinging bites make life unbearable for weeks on end. "When they arise they come by the hundreds of thousands and leave no patch of skin unbloodied," writes biologist Bernd Heinrich. "They hover about in gray clouds that are sometimes so thick you hesitate to inhale deeply. . . . I don't begrudge them. They are part of the bargain. It is these tiny creatures that help keep Maine green, by keeping people out." ■

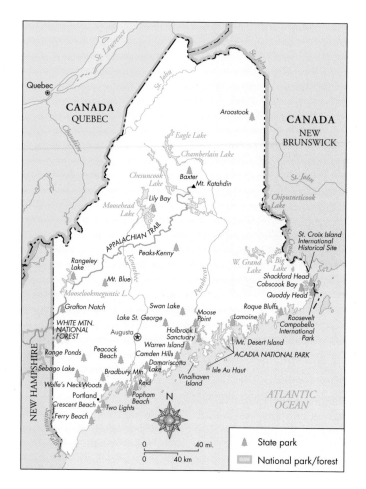

Maine's parks and forests

cling to the trunks and branches of trees, usually in deep, damp woods. They produce flowers of stunning beauty. Fifteen of Maine's orchid species are in danger of extinction.

For centuries, Maine's coastal waters have been a rich fishing ground. Ocean fish include herring, cod, flounder, and sharks. Hair seals, whales, and porpoises sometimes frolic offshore. The most famous of Maine's sea creatures is, of course, the lobster. Lobsters were once so plentiful that they washed ashore during storms and heaped up on the beaches in great snapping piles. Today, lobstering is a major industry. Half of all the lobsters marketed in the United States come from Maine waters.

Long, Cold Winters

In January 1998, two disastrous blizzards struck Maine back to back. Tree limbs crashed under the weight of the snow, severing telephone and power lines. Schools closed and businesses shut down. Snowbound families ran out of food. TV and radio stations lost transmission. For three weeks, some 400,000 Mainers were cut off from one another and from the rest of the world.

Such severe conditions are extreme, even for Maine, but Main-

ers are used to long, hard winters. Maine is farther north than Iceland, and its shores are washed by the frigid Labrador Current. The average temperature in January is 15° F (−9°C). Northern Maine receives almost twice as much snow as does the southern coast.

In Maine, summer comes late and does not last long. In June, the flowers bloom and the birds rush to build nests and raise their young. In July, visitors pack the parks and beaches, lapping up the sunshine. By the end of August, the leaves begin to change color, and in October Mainers put on their heavy socks and mufflers once again.

Fortunately, Maine winters bring their own special pleasures. There is plenty of ice for skating and hockey. There is snow for

Maine winters are usually long and bitterly cold.

Opposite: The short
summers are often
enjoyed on Maine's
beaches.

Long Live the Earmuff!

With its cold climate, it is no wonder that Maine is the birthplace of a winter necessity most of us take for granted—earmuffs. The world's first earmuffs were designed in 1873 by Chester Greenwood, a fifteen-year-old boy from Farmington. Greenwood patented his invention in 1876, and earmuffs earned him a steady living for the rest of his days. Every January, Farmington celebrates Chester Greenwood Day in honor of the man who has spared millions of people from suffering frostbite. ■

sledding, skiing, and old-fashioned snowball fights. And every now and then, the night sky explodes in a dazzling display of dancing colors, the aurora borealis, or northern lights. The northern lights are caused by electrical charges in the atmosphere of the far north. They are a frequent phenomenon beyond the Arctic Circle, but sometimes this stunning natural light show travels as far south as northern Maine.

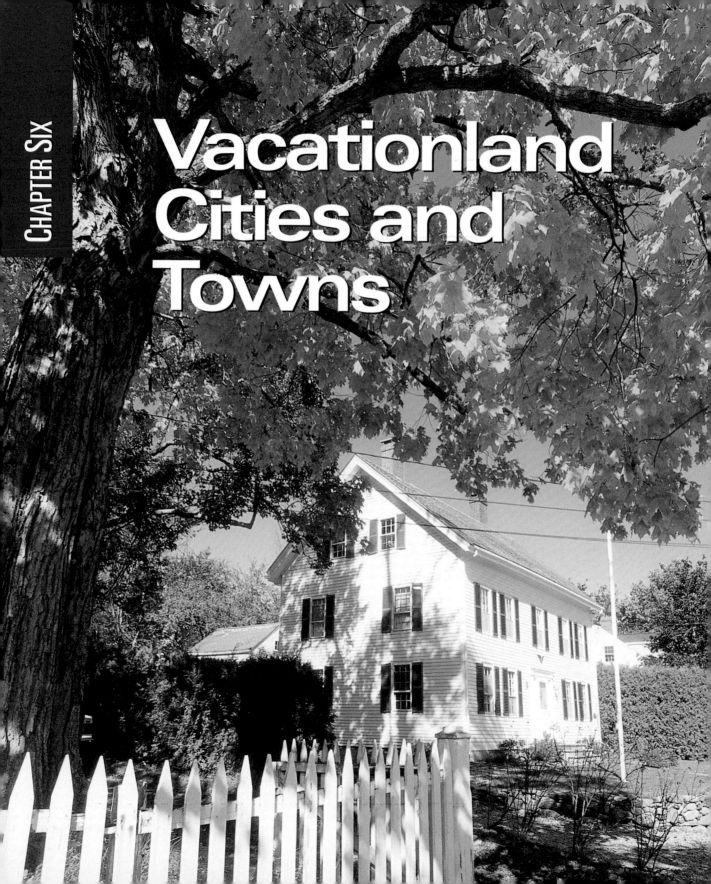

CHAPTER SIX

Vacationland Cities and Towns

The coastal town of Bucksport

Most visitors are lured to Maine by its seashores. Others come to fish the streams or to hunt in the north woods. Few outsiders realize that Maine is dotted with fascinating towns and small cities. These towns have almost as much to offer as Maine's great outdoors.

Harbors and Cottages

The fishing and shipbuilding industries gave rise to many of the towns along Maine's jagged coast. Today another industry, tourism, helps keep these communities alive. Though the ocean is usually too cold for swimming, visitors find plenty of other things to do.

The South Coast

Kittery is sometimes described as "exurbia." It is a commuter town though it lies well beyond the suburbs that ring Boston. Exiles from Boston began to buy homes in Kittery in the early

Opposite: Castine, near the Penobscot Bay Peninsula

1980s. Each day they commute 100 miles (160 km) or more to their jobs in and around the big city.

Kittery was once a major shipbuilding center. Now it bristles with condominiums, factory outlets, and shopping malls. Several stately old homes are reminders of its seagoing past. Palladian is the 1760 mansion of Lady Pepperrell. Her husband, Sir William Pepperrell, captured the French stronghold of Louisbourg in Quebec during the French and Indian Wars.

The towns of Kennebunk and Kennebunkport are often referred to as the Kennebunks. Kennebunkport is a resort community with many splendid mansions from the late nineteenth century. The family of former U.S. president George Bush has had a summer home at Walker's Point in Kennebunkport since 1903. While Bush was in office (1989–1993) the town became nationally famous as the presidential retreat. Kennebunkport's Seashore Trolley Museum has a unique collection of some 200 trolley cars from all over the world. Not far from town is the Rachel Carson National Wildlife Refuge, a pocket of untamed woodland surrounded by condos, malls, and motels.

Kennebunk, a few miles inland, is much less geared toward the tourist trade, but it

The Wedding Cake House is one of Kennebunk's attractions.

The Edge of the Sea

Rachel Carson (1907–1964) spent many summers on the Maine coast. She was fascinated by plants and animals and was a careful observer of the natural world. Carson's first book, *The Edge of the Sea* (1941), reflects the many hours she spent peering into tide pools along the Maine shore. Shortly before her death in 1962 Carson published her most influential book, *Silent Spring* (1962). In that book, she warned that pollution from pesticides and other chemicals posed a serious threat to animals and people. Carson's work heightened public awareness of the dangers of pollution and led to the passage of laws designed to protect the environment for humans and animals alike. ■

has one of the most frequently photographed historic houses in the state. Kennebunk's famous Wedding Cake House was completed in 1856 by George Bourne, a retired sea captain. Bourne covered the house and barn with elaborate wood carvings that look like the creations of a fancy-cake designer.

Portland and Beyond

The largest city in Maine, Portland is often ranked as one of the most livable cities in the United States. Its most upscale neighborhood, Prout's Neck, is famous for its elegant old houses. Portland is home to an acclaimed symphony orchestra and to several excellent theaters. Its City Hall Auditorium has hosted organ concerts since 1918.

Portland has a number of handsomely restored historic homes, including the Wadsworth Longfellow House, built in 1785. Its first owner, Peleg Wadsworth, was the grandfather of poet William

Portland has many appealing neighborhoods, including its historic districts.

Wadsworth Longfellow. Longfellow spent many happy summers in this house when he was growing up. Many of his letters and other keepsakes are there on display. Another historic house belonged to Neal Dow, who helped pass Maine's first temperance law in 1851. When Dow ran for the office of mayor in Portland his opponents said that his slogan ought to be, "Water, water everywhere, but not a drop to drink!" Nevertheless, Dow won the election. Later, he became a Union general in the Civil War.

A landmark of downtown Portland is Monument Square. Since

Founding Fathers

The first European to settle on the site of present-day Portland was Christopher Levett, who arrived in 1623. With a small company of followers Levett built a stone house on an island in Casco Bay. After his first Maine winter he felt he had seen enough of the New World, and returned hastily to England. Around 1630, two businessmen, George Cleeve and Richard Tucker, established a lasting settlement on the mainland. Their settlement grew into the present-day city of Portland. Over the years, Portland has been known by many names. They include Machigonne, Elbow, The Neck, Casco, and Falmouth. The city acquired the name *Portland* around the time of the American Revolution, and has been that ever since. ■

the American Revolution the square has been a local gathering place. The monument for which the square is known was created in 1891 by Maine sculptor Charles Simmons as a memorial to Maine soldiers who served in the Civil War.

South of Portland begins "Kidz Alley," a 10-mile (16-km) stretch of water parks and amusement parks. This area includes the Children's Museum of Maine and the Maine Aquarium. Old Orchard Beach is a 7-mile (11-km) strip of sandy shore dotted with concessions and rides.

Just up the coast from Portland is Brunswick, home to Bowdoin College since 1794. The Bowdoin Museum of Art has a fine collection of paintings by artists who worked in Maine,

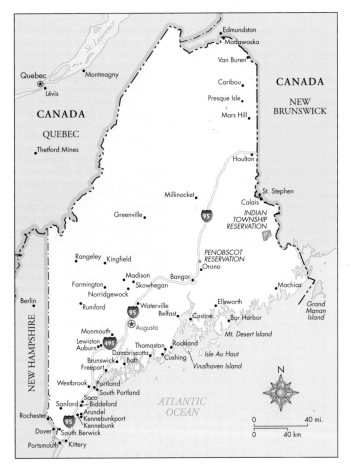

Maine's cities and interstates

including Andrew Wyeth, John Singer Sargent, and Winslow Homer. The Naval Air Station at Brunswick is a major submarine base for the U.S. Navy.

In the late 1800s, Bar Harbor was like a gala summer festival each year. Visitors crowded the beaches and boardwalks, enjoying the sun and salt air. In the 1930s, when few Americans could

Thar She Blows!

Just as some people enjoy bird-watching, others like to watch whales. Bar Harbor maintains a small but active whale-watching fleet. Boats carry visitors out to sea on expeditions to sight and photograph the great beasts. Like the whalers of old, whale-watchers search the horizon for the telltale spout of spray as a whale surfaces and takes a breath. Sometimes whales travel alone; sometimes they move in groups called pods. Either way, these immense creatures are always a spectacular sight. ■

afford to take vacations, the town declined. Then, in 1947, a disastrous fire swept through Bar Harbor. Fortunately, the flames spared many of the town's finest old houses. In the 1980s, Bar Harbor began to make a comeback. Many visitors stop here on their way to Acadia National Park.

In the years before the American Revolution, a French nobleman, Baron de St. Castine, settled on the Maine coast. According to some accounts, the baron married a Penobscot princess and was accepted as a chief by her people. The lovely coastal town of Castine is named for him. Castine has many elegant nineteenth-century homes graced by towering elm trees. Most U.S. towns lost their elms between the 1930s and 1960s to a parasite that caused Dutch elm disease, but the citizens of Castine have managed to keep their elm trees alive and healthy.

The town of Castine was named for Baron de St. Castine.

Castine's Fort George stands as a reminder of the War of 1812 (1812–1815), when the United States and Great Britain fought for control of the high seas. During the war, the British occupied the fort for eight months. A series of panels on the fort's walls tell the story in pictures. Castine's Wilson Museum features Native American crafts as well as artifacts from Maine's prehistoric peoples. It also has one of the most unusual exhibits in any U.S. museum—a collection of nineteenth- and twentieth-century hearses!

Towns Upriver

In the past, rivers played a crucial role in Maine's economy. Not surprisingly many inland towns grew up along the banks of the Kennebec, the Androscoggin, and the Penobscot.

Up the Kennebec

Augusta on the Kennebec has served as Maine's capital since 1832. The original capitol was designed by the famous architect Charles Bulfinch, who also created the Massachusetts State House in Boston. Maine's capitol has undergone many renovations, but Bulfinch's columned facade has been preserved. The capitol is part of a complex of buildings including the State Library and the State Museum. The Maine State Museum has a wide variety of historical exhibits. A favorite with visitors is the Lion, a steam engine that hauled loads of lumber to the sawmills from 1846 until 1901.

Augusta's Fort Western is a legacy of the French and Indian Wars. When threatened with enemy attack, the colonists took

Tilbury Town

The little town of Gardiner was the boyhood home of poet Edward Arlington Robinson (1869–1935). Robinson immortalized Gardiner as "Tilbury Town" in some of his most famous poems. His work reveals the secrets and disappointments behind many ordinary lives. In "Miniver Cheevy," Robinson describes a man who longs to do knightly deeds, though his life is empty and sad. He concludes:

> *Miniver Cheevy, born too late,*
> *Scratched his head and kept on thinking;*
> *Miniver coughed and called it fate,*
> *And kept on drinking.*

A boat-building demonstration at Fort Western

refuge within its walls. Later, the fort became a dormitory for Irish immigrants who worked in the textile mills. Today, it is staffed by men and women who wear colonial costumes and demonstrate colonial crafts. Visitors get hands-on experience in weaving, sheepshearing, and cooking over an open fire.

Mission to the Indians

In 1694, a French Jesuit missionary named Father Sebastien Rasles opened a mission to serve Native Americans at Norridgewock, near what is now Waterville. Rasles spent the next thirty years converting the Indians to Roman Catholicism and teaching them to read and write. His dictionary of the Abenaki language is still a resource for those interested in Native American cultures. ■

May the Force Be with You

On a hill above the town of Rangeley stands Orgonon, once the estate of eccentric psychologist Wilhelm Reich (1897–1957). Born in Austria, Reich studied for a time under the psychoanalyst Sigmund Freud. Reich disagreed sharply with Freud and other analysts, and left Europe to explore his own radical ideas. He moved to Rangeley in 1948. There he conducted experiments to prove his theory that an energy force he called "orgone" controlled the universe. Reich invented an assortment of machines for capturing and harnessing orgone. Among his machines was a "cloudbuster," which he claimed could produce storms.

When Reich began to sell his inventions around the country, he was convicted of fraud in interstate commerce. He died in a federal penitentiary, and was buried on the Orgonon grounds. Many of Reich's inventions are displayed at Orgonon. Visitors must decide for themselves whether he was a genius, a crackpot, or a threat to national security. ■

Colby College in Waterville

Colby College was founded in the town of Waterville in 1813. The college's art museum has a fine collection of twentieth-century paintings and sculpture. One of Colby's most famous graduates was Elijah Parrish Lovejoy (1802–1837), a journalist and a staunch supporter of the abolitionist movement. Lovejoy was murdered by a mob in Alton, Illinois, for editing an outspoken antislavery newspaper.

Along the Androscoggin

The towns of Lewiston and Auburn face each other across the Androscoggin River. They are linked by the Longley Memorial Bridge. Lewiston's Peter and Paul Church, with its distinctive twin towers, is the second-largest

Living in the Past

The Norlands Living History Center at Livermore is not a museum —it is a journey into the past. Each visitor is given the name and role of someone in a farm family of the 1870s. Then each person puts on typical clothing of the era and helps with chores in the house, barn, and fields. Children attend a real one-room schoolhouse, where they recite in unison and write their lessons with chalk on slates. In the evening, everyone eats by lantern light and sits around the fire sharing stories. After three days, visitors appreciate the hardships and pleasures of life more than a century ago. ■

church in New England. Each year, Lewiston's Bates College hosts a dance festival that has earned national recognition.

In the late nineteenth century, many factory owners from Lewiston and Auburn built homes in nearby Monmouth. They also graced Monmouth with a beautiful opera house called Cumston Hall. Today, Cumston Hall hosts many concerts at low prices, making them accessible to people from all walks of life.

Up the Penobscot

Searsport, near the mouth of the Penobscot River, was a major shipbuilding center in the nineteenth century. Today, the town's claim to fame is the Penobscot Marine Museum. The museum embraces several historic buildings, including the homes of three sea captains. Through maps and charts, antique navigational instruments, ship models, and photographs, the displays recapture the days of the sailing ships. But one special exhibit has nothing to do with life at sea. It is the world's largest collection of glass butter dishes!

When Henry Thoreau made his famous canoe trips in the 1840s, he bought supplies in Bangor before heading upriver. In Thoreau's day, Bangor was the northernmost outpost of civilization. It was the town where logging crews brought raw timber to be shipped to sawmills downstream and where they gathered fresh supplies for their next trip into the back country.

Today, Bangor shops are still outfitting backpackers, logging crews, and anyone else headed into the north woods. The city is also a leading commercial center for the people who live farther north. Some customers travel nearly 100 miles (160 km) to shop at Bangor's malls. Bangor also provides the area with culture and entertainment. The Bangor Symphony is the second-oldest continuously operating symphony orchestra in the United States. It gave its first performance in 1896.

The University of Maine was established at Orono in 1862. The college brings a wide array of cultural events to this otherwise quiet town. Few other communities in the state enjoy such a lively schedule of plays, concerts, and dance programs. The university also maintains a planetarium and a small museum of anthropology.

Stevens Hall at the University of Maine

The North Woods

The towns in northern Maine are small and widely scattered. Most are involved in the pulp or timber industries. Tourism, too, is an important part of life in this thinly populated region. Many visitors stop in these northern towns to be outfitted for fishing or hunting expeditions.

Greenville lies at the southern tip of Moosehead Lake. Displays at the Moosehead Marine Museum trace the lake's history as a resort area. The S.S. *Katahdin* is a diesel-operated boat that carries visitors on two-hour tours of the lake. When it was built in 1914, the *Katahdin* was powered by steam.

Houlton was at the heart of the Aroostook War of 1839, in which Maine and New Brunswick, Canada, went to arms in a border dispute. Today, Houlton is a peaceful agricultural center with many charming nineteenth-century homes.

Each July, the quiet town of Caribou springs to life with the annual Crown of Maine Balloon Festival. Balloonists from all over the country flock to Caribou and take to the air. Caribou's Nylander Museum has exhibits on the state's geology and archaeology and an extensive collection of artifacts of the Red Paint people.

Where the Aroostook River and the Presque Isle Stream come together stands the town of Presque Isle. Residents like to say it is "almost an island" because of its location on the two waterways. Presque Isle was an important air base during World War II when planes took off from its airstrip bound for Britain. Today, the town's biggest annual event is the Northern Maine Fair held each August. The fair is a week-long extravaganza of games, square dancing, and delicious food of every variety. Judges award prizes

Opposite: Greenville lies along Moosehead Lake.

for the year's finest horses, cattle, and pigs. Farmers outdo each other, displaying bigger and better pumpkins, cucumbers, and cabbages. And, of course, there are potatoes, the heaviest and tastiest that Maine can produce. The most popular event of the fair, however, is a series of harness races. Drivers perched in lightweight carriages called sulkies urge their horses to breakneck speeds. Most of the drivers are local farmers, and each has a loyal band of cheering fans.

Opposite: Costumed guides at Acadian Historic Village

Many people who live in and around Van Buren are of French-Canadian heritage. The Acadian Historic Village outside Van Buren pays tribute to French-Canadian history and culture. The village contains sixteen fully restored or reconstructed buildings that reveal how French Canadians lived in the eighteenth and nineteenth centuries.

The northernmost town in Maine is Madawaska on the St. John River. Though it is surrounded by forests and farmland, Madawaska is a heavily industrial community. Huge factories transform liquid wood pulp into several kinds of paper. The smell of pulp constantly hangs in the air, but residents accept the smell as part of life. The paper mills create a product that is in demand, and provide jobs to the people of the region. Every June, Madawaska hosts the annual Acadian Festival—a rollicking celebration of music, food, and good fellowship.

CHAPTER SEVEN

From Town Meetings to the Capitol

Inside the capitol

People in Maine have a firsthand relationship with their government. Because the state's population is so small, Mainers are often personally acquainted with their representatives, whether they serve on the town council or in the state legislature. Mainers have the opportunity to express their feelings about current issues to officials who can make a difference. It is only fitting that Maine's state motto is "*Dirigo*," meaning "I lead" or "I direct," in Latin.

Of the People, by the People

In 1819, a group of men gathered at the First Parish Unitarian Church in Portland. They were delegates to Maine's first and only Constitutional Convention. The body of laws they wrote has been changed, or amended, more than 150 times since it was officially adopted in 1820, but it has never been completely rewritten. Maine still operates under its original state constitution.

Maine's constitution modeled the state government upon the federal government of the United States. The government of Maine has three branches. The executive branch, or office of the governor, ensures that the laws are carried out. The legislative branch, or state legislature, makes and repeals laws. The judicial branch, or court system, interprets or explains the laws.

The governor is the only official in Maine who is chosen by means of a statewide election. Maine has no lieutenant governor.

Opposite: The state capitol at Augusta

Maine's State Government

Executive Branch

Governor

Secretary of State | State Treasurer | Attorney General | Auditor

Legislative Branch

Senate | House of Representatives

Judicial Branch

Supreme Court

Superior Court

District Courts

Probate Courts

The Maine senate chamber

Maine's Governors

Name	Party	Term	Name	Party	Term
William King	Dem.	1820–1821	Harris M. Plaisted	Dem.	1881–1883
William D. Williamson	Dem.	1821	Frederick Robie	Rep.	1883–1887
Benjamin Ames	Dem.	1821–1822	Joseph R. Bodwell	Rep.	1887
Albion K. Parris	Dem.	1822–1827	S. S. Marble	Rep.	1887–1889
Enoch Lincoln	Dem.	1827–1829	Edwin C. Burleigh	Rep.	1889–1893
Nathan Cutler	Dem.	1829–1830	Henry B. Cleaves	Rep.	1893–1897
Joshua Hall	Dem.	1830	Llewellyn Powers	Rep.	1897–1901
Jonathan Hunton	Nat. Rep.	1830–1831	John Fremont Hill	Rep.	1901–1905
Samuel E. Smith	Dem.	1831–1834	William T. Cobb	Rep.	1905–1909
Robert Dunlap	Dem.	1834–1838	Bert M. Fernald	Rep.	1909–1911
Edward Kent	Whig	1838–1839	Frederick W. Plaisted	Dem.	1911–1913
John Fairfield	Dem.	1839–1841	William T. Haines	Rep.	1913–1915
Edward Kent	Whig	1841–1842	Oakley C. Curtis	Dem.	1915–1917
John Fairfield	Dem.	1842–1843	Carl E. Milliken	Rep.	1917–1921
Edward Kavanagh	Dem.	1843–1844	Frederic H. Parkhurst	Rep.	1921
Hugh J. Anderson	Dem.	1844–1847	Percival P. Baxter	Rep.	1921–1925
John W. Dana	Dem.	1847–1850	Ralph Owen Brewster	Rep.	1925–1929
John Hubbard	Dem.	1850–1853	William Tudor Gardiner	Rep.	1929–1933
William G. Crosby	Whig	1853–1855	Louis J. Brann	Dem.	1933–1937
Anson P. Morrill	Rep.	1855–1856	Lewis O. Barrows	Rep.	1937–1941
Samuel Wells	Dem.	1856–1857	Sumner Sewall	Rep.	1941–1945
Hannibal Hamlin	Rep.	1857	Horace A. Hildreth	Rep.	1945–1949
Joseph H. Williams	Rep.	1857–1858	Frederick G. Payne	Rep.	1949–1952
Lot M. Morrill	Rep.	1858–1861	Burton M. Cross	Rep.	1952–1955
Israel Washburn Jr.	Rep.	1861–1863	Edmund S. Muskie	Dem.	1955–1959
Abner Coburn	Rep.	1863–1864	Robert Haskell	Rep.	1959
Samuel Cony	Rep.	1864–1867	Clinton Clauson	Dem.	1959
Joshua L. Chamberlain	Rep.	1867–1871	John H. Reed	Rep.	1959–1967
Sidney Perham	Rep.	1871–1874	Kenneth M. Curtis	Dem.	1967–1975
Nelson Dingley Jr.	Rep.	1874–1876	James B. Longley	Ind.	1975–1979
Seldon Connor	Rep.	1876–1879	Joseph E. Brennan	Dem.	1979–1987
Alonzo Garcelon	Dem.	1879–1880	John R. McKernan Jr.	Rep.	1987–1995
Daniel F. Davis	Rep.	1880–1881	Angus King	Ind.	1995–

State Flag and Seal

Adopted in 1909, Maine's flag bears many symbols of the state's long history. Against a blue background, two figures support a shield emblazoned with the state seal. One of the figures is a farmer with a scythe, representing Maine's long commitment to agriculture. The other figure is a sailor leaning on a ship's anchor, a symbol of Maine's connection with the sea. On the seal are pictured a moose and a pine tree, representing the state's forests. The figures and the seal are under the North Star. In the days of the sailing ships, the North Star was a guiding light for sailors lost at sea. ■

Maine's counties

The governor may not serve more than two consecutive four-year terms. He or she can veto any bill that has been passed by the legislature, but the legislature can override the governor's veto with a two-thirds vote in each house.

Like most states, Maine has a two-chambered legislature. The senate, or upper house, has 35 elected members. Mainers elect 151 members to the house of representatives, or lower house. The legislature meets at the state capitol in Augusta for regular sessions that begin each January. It elects several members of the governor's cabinet, a group of officials who advise the governor on important state matters. Among these cabinet members are the secretary of state, attorney general, and state treasurer.

Maine's district courts handle a variety of minor civil and criminal cases. A person charged with committing a serious crime, or felony, is taken before the superior court. The superior court has sixteen judges. The state's highest court is the supreme court in Augusta. Its chief justice and six associate justices are appointed by the governor for seven-year terms. The supreme court makes final decisions in both civil and criminal cases from throughout the state.

A proposed amendment to the constitution must pass the legislature with a two-thirds vote. The amendment then goes directly to the people. To become law, a constitutional amendment must receive a majority of the popular vote.

Maine's state government helps support public schools, libraries, hospitals, museums, highways, and many other services and programs. About half of the state's revenue comes from taxes. The remainder comes in the form of grants from the federal government. Mainers have paid a state income tax since 1969. They also pay a sales tax and special taxes on cigarettes and alcohol. Maine has kept its

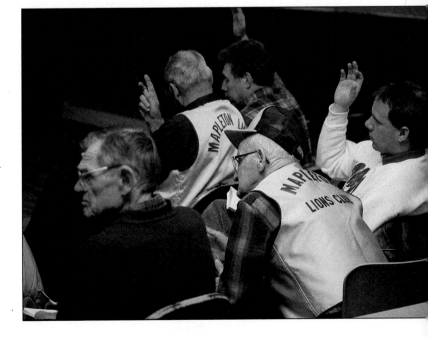

Town meetings are one form of government in Maine.

Maine's State Symbols

State bird: Black-capped chickadee This little bird is both lively and hardy. It does not fly south in the fall and seems to stay cheerful through the bitter Maine winters.

State animal: Moose (left) With its spectacular rack of antlers, which may weigh up to 50 pounds (23 kg), the bull moose is a coveted trophy for hunters. By 1935, hunting and logging had almost wiped out Maine's moose population. Moose hunting was outlawed from 1935 until 1980. Today, the moose is prized by both hunters and wildlife watchers.

State fish: Landlocked salmon The landlocked salmon is a cousin of the mighty salmon that swims upriver to spawn each year. But, instead of making fantastic journeys, the landlocked salmon lives out its life in a quiet lake. Landlocked salmon are fierce fighters and highly prized by sports fishers.

State insect: Honeybee (left) By long tradition, many farmers in Maine set up beehives and harvest honey each fall. Beekeepers suffered a severe setback in the 1990s when a virus wiped out many honey-producing swarms.

State tree: White pine The trunk of the white pine made splendid masts in the days of sailing ships. Coastal towns such as Freeport still have long, straight main streets, dating from a time when 100-foot (31-m) masts were carried from the mills to the boatbuilders on the shore without turning.

State fossil: *Pertica quadriferia* Fossilized remains of this ancient plant have been found in marshes near Mount Katahdin. Fossils dating back 400 million years are on display at the State Museum in Augusta.

State mineral: Tourmaline (below) Sought by jewelers and collectors, tourmaline is found in deposits of silica in western Maine. It comes in a variety of colors including black, brownish-black, blue, and green. Sometimes it is almost clear. ■

corporate taxes fairly low to attract businesses.

On the local level, Maine is divided into sixteen counties. Aroostook County, covering 6,453 square miles (16,713 sq km), is the largest U.S. county east of the Mississippi River. It is as big as the states of Connecticut and Rhode Island combined.

Twenty-two communities within the state of Maine are designated as cities. Another 434 are classified as towns. Following a long-standing New England tradition, many Maine towns hold regular town meetings. Residents raise their concerns, make suggestions, and vote on issues that affect their lives. The town meeting is an example of true democracy at work.

About half of the land in Maine is unincorporated—it is not part of any town or city. Most of this unincorporated land belongs to private pulp and timber companies.

Maine's State Song
"State of Maine Song"

Words and music by Roger Vinton Snow

O Pine Tree State,
Your woods, fields, and hills,
Your lakes, streams, and rock-bound coast
Will ever fill our hearts with thrills.
And tho' we seek far and wide,
Our search will be in vain
To find a fairer spot on Earth
Than Maine! Maine! Maine!

Party Lines

When the Republican Party was founded in 1854, its main issue was opposition to slavery. Because antislavery sentiment was strong in Maine, it became a solid Republican state. For nearly 100 years, Maine held staunchly to its Republican loyalties. On a few occasions, Democratic candidates were elected governor, but they seldom lasted more than one term. For the most part, the only elections that mattered were the Republican primaries, in which the party chose its candidates for the general election.

The Woman with the Red, Red Rose

In 1940, Margaret Chase Smith (1897–1995) of Skowhegan entered the U.S. Congress to serve out the term of her deceased husband. Smith was re-elected to the U.S. House of Representatives four times. When she won a seat in the U.S. Senate in 1948, she became the first woman ever to serve in both houses of Congress. Before the presidential election of 1964, Smith made a serious bid for the Republican nomination. She was the first woman ever to seek the nomination of a major party in a presidential election. At public appearances, Margaret Chase Smith usually wore a big red rose. The red rose became her personal trademark to the media. ■

During the Great Depression of the 1930s, the Democratic Party gained a following in Maine for the first time. Louis J. Brann, a Democrat, was elected governor in 1932 and served two terms. However, in 1936, Maine and Vermont were the only two states that voted not to re-elect the popular Democratic president, Franklin D. Roosevelt.

In 1954, Maine chose another Democratic governor—Edmund S. Muskie. Over the years that followed, Maine evolved to become a thoroughly two-party state. In the late 1990s, 33 percent of all Mainers were registered as Democrats and 30 percent were Republicans. The remaining 37 percent claimed no specific party.

In 1994, Mainers elected Angus King to serve as governor. King was only the second Independent candidate ever elected to this office in the state's history. As an Independent candidate, King claimed no party allegiance.

The Senator from Rumford

As a boy growing up in Rumford, Maine, Edmund Muskie (1914–1996) was unusually shy. But somehow he overcame his shyness to make politics his lifelong career. Mainers elected Muskie to serve as governor in 1954. In 1958 Muskie won a seat in the U.S. Senate, becoming the first Democratic senator in Maine's history.

When Democrat Hubert Humphrey of Minnesota ran for president in 1968, he selected Edmund Muskie as his running mate. Humphrey and Muskie were defeated by Richard M. Nixon and Spiro Agnew. Muskie served briefly as secretary of state under President Jimmy Carter in 1980 and 1981. ■

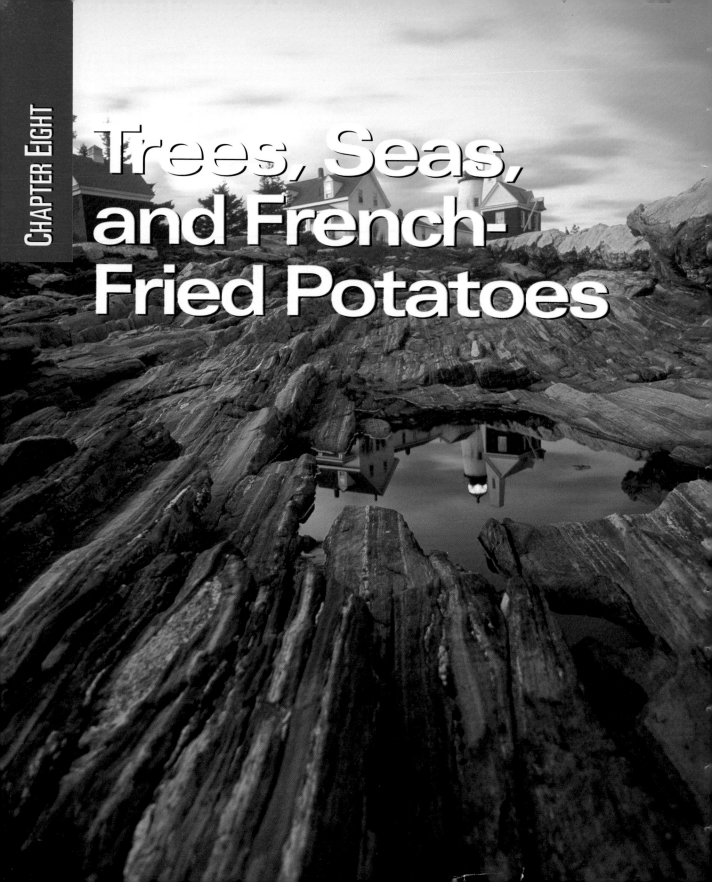

CHAPTER EIGHT

Trees, Seas, and French-Fried Potatoes

The logging industry continues to be a vital part of Maine's economy.

I t is no accident that Mainers chose the white pine to be their state tree. The white pine was once the mainstay of the state's economy. Though this magnificent tree has nearly disappeared, the forest is still a major factor in the economy of Maine. Fishing, farming, manufacturing, and service industries also play crucial roles.

Riches from the Forest

A hiker who set out for the Canadian border from the town of Millinocket would trek through nearly 100 miles (160 km) of forest. However, this vast stretch of forested land is not part of any park or wildlife preserve. Most of it belongs to powerful pulp and timber companies. These companies harvest the trees much as a farmer harvests corn or wheat.

Pulp and timber companies have purchased about 10 million acres (4 million ha) of land in northern Maine. They cut most of Maine's native trees including maple, ash, white and yellow birch, beech, oak, spruce, hemlock, fir, and white pine. Forests are a renewable resource—when trees are cut down, new trees can be planted. Timber companies do plant trees to rebuild the forests they cut down. But forests grow very slowly, over decades or even centuries. Many people feel that Maine's original forests can never be replaced.

Opposite: Pemaquid Point Lighthouse

Trees, Seas, and French-Fried Potatoes **95**

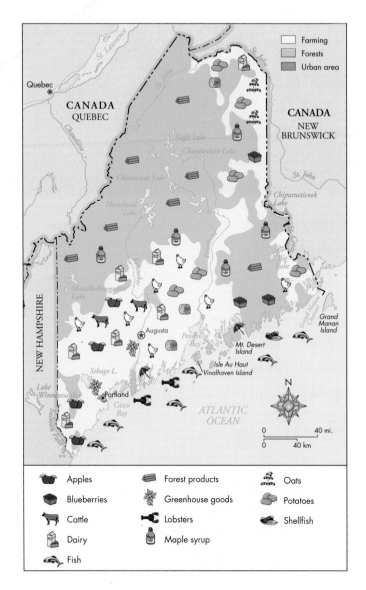

☐	Farming	
▨	Forests	
■	Urban area	

Apples
Blueberries
Cattle
Dairy
Fish

Forest products
Greenhouse goods
Lobsters
Maple syrup

Oats
Potatoes
Shellfish

Maine's natural resources

The pulp and timber industries create jobs for at least 10,000 people in Maine. Some Mainers work in the woods, operating chain saws, cranes, and other heavy equipment. Some work in sawmills where logs are turned into boards. Still others are employed by paper mills, converting wood pulp into various grades of paper.

Logging is not the only commercial use of Maine's forests. Maine ranks third in the nation in the production of maple sugar and syrup. Some sugar comes from "sap orchards," where sugar maples are planted and tended. Sugar is still taken from wild trees too.

Like maple syrup, blueberries are a perfect addition to steaming hot pancakes. And, like sugar maple trees, blueberry bushes grow wild in Maine. About half of the wild blueberries sold in the United States are harvested from Maine's woods and wetlands. Harvested by special rakes, blueberries are also produced commercially by Maine farmers. All in all, Maine leads the world in blueberry production.

From the Farmer's Fields

Before the American Revolution, Scotch-Irish immigrants brought one of their favorite food crops to Maine—the potato. According to some accounts, Mainers rejected the potato at first. Since it was mentioned nowhere in the Bible, they argued that it could not be a wholesome food. But potatoes grew well in Maine's river valleys, and soon the crop caught on. By 1820, when Maine became a state, potatoes were its leading crop. With improved shipping and storage methods, Maine potatoes found markets all over the country.

After World War II, Americans developed a passion for French fries. Whether they came from fresh potatoes or from a frozen package, French fries made some Maine farmers rich.

Harvesting potatoes in Houlton

The Fashionable Spud

In the early decades of the twentieth century, Americans fell in love with stiffly starched collars and cuffs. For generations, Mainers had been using potato starch to make their clothes look crisp and fresh. When the new fashion struck, people found that potato starch was just what they needed to keep them in style. Demand for potato starch soared beyond the potato growers' wildest dreams. For a time, Maine produced 90 percent of the potato starch used in the United States, all in the interest of fashion. ■

Maine farms produce cattle as well as produce.

Today, Maine is the leading potato producer in New England, and ranks eighth in potato production in the nation. Most potato farms are in the northern part of the state in Aroostook County and the St. John River Valley.

In addition to potatoes, Maine farms produce apples, cranberries, eggs, and dairy products. Dairy and beef cattle are raised chiefly in the south-central portion of the state. Chicken farmers in Maine produce thousands of broilers each year.

What Maine Grows, Manufactures, and Mines

Agriculture

Potatoes
Eggs
Milk

Manufacturing

Paper products
Wood products
Transportation equipment
Electrical equipment
Leather products
Food products

Mining

Sand and gravel

From the Sea

Every day, giant fishing boats unload their scaly catch on the wharves of Portland, Rockland, and other coastal cities. Maine ranks eighth among the states in the production of ocean fish, and fourth in shellfish production. No other state brings in as many lobsters. Flounder, halibut, and shrimp are also important ocean harvests.

Until the middle of the twentieth century, fishing and lobstering were mainly family businesses. Fathers passed their boats and fishing gear on to their children. But in the 1950s and 1960s, fishing became a big business. Huge trawlers cruised the Maine coast, spreading miles of nets to bring in tons of fish at a time. Lobstering crews carpeted the ocean floor with their lobster traps. Few family businesses could compete. The advent of "big

Catch of the Day

Lobsters walk along the ocean floor, feeding on clams, crabs, or anything else they can find. Lobster fishers lower cagelike traps, baited with chunks of meat or fish, to the sea floor. Each lobster crew marks its own traps with colored buoys. Environmentalists fear that heavy lobstering will dangerously deplete the population of these tasty crustaceans. But lobster fishers argue that they are actually enhancing the environment. They claim they are feeding a host of fish and other sea creatures by putting so much bait into the ocean. ■

fishing" ended a way of life that had survived in Maine for more than three centuries.

From the Factories

Most people think of Maine as a state of farms and forests. Actually, agriculture accounts for only 2 percent of Maine's gross state product (GSP), the total sum of all goods and services produced in the state. Twenty-three percent of the GSP comes from manufacturing. Maine has been producing textiles since the beginning of

Full Speed Ahead!

Among the first developers of the automobile were the Stanley brothers—identical twins born in Kingfield, Maine. Francis Edgar Stanley (1849–1918) and Freelan Oscar Stanley (1849–1940) built their first steam-powered car in 1897. They sold their famous "Stanley Steamers" until Francis's death in a high-speed auto crash.

From the beginning of their career, the Stanleys wanted to build fast cars. In 1906, one of their automobiles reached a dizzying velocity of 128 mph (206 kph). Some of the Stanleys' creations are now on display at the Stanley Museum in Kingfield. The museum also contains photographs, models, and other memorabilia of the brothers' lives and work. ■

A paper mill on the Androscoggin River

the nineteenth century. Maine factories also turn out shoes, electrical equipment, and processed foods.

Not surprisingly, the biggest industry in Maine is the manufacture of paper. International Paper, Scott Paper, and several other paper companies are based in the state. Paper accounts for 43 percent of Maine's manufactured goods.

Doing Things for Others

About 75 percent of Maine's GSP comes from service industries. People in service industries provide services for others. Service workers include doctors, lawyers, beauticians, teachers, bankers, retail salespeople, and bus drivers.

One of the largest of Maine's service industries is tourism. People in the tourist industry work in hotels, shops, museums, parks, restaurants, and government offices. Tourism has been important to Maine's economy since the late nineteenth century. Maine is a getaway place for people from the congested cities and suburbs along the Eastern Seaboard. Summer crowds flock to Bar Harbor, Ogunquit, Kennebunkport, and other resort communities along the coast. Maine's lakes and rivers attract fishing and boat-

Need a Toothpick?

Lumber and paper are not the only products made from Maine's timber. Maine factories produce a host of wood and paper products, from packing crates to matchsticks. Whenever you open a box of toothpicks, the chances are that they came from a factory in Maine. Maine is known as the Toothpick Capital of the World. ■

Oh Four Oh Three Three

Leon Leonwood Bean (1872–1967) grew up in Oxford County, Maine, where he loved to go hiking and hunting. To his annoyance, he could never find boots that kept his feet dry when he was out in the woods. In 1905, Bean and his brother opened a store in the coastal town of Freeport. Soon, Bean began to experiment with shoe design, developing a rubber-soled boot that was sturdy and waterproof. He marketed his "Bean boots" chiefly through mail-order catalogues. Over the years, the L. L. Bean Company added a wide variety of sportswear and related items. In 1951, Bean decided to keep the store open 24 hours a day. A customer can walk in at 3 A.M. and talk to a salesperson about hiking shoes or thermal socks.

For decades, L. L. Bean was known chiefly to outdoor enthusiasts. But in the 1970s, L. L. Bean clothes suddenly became fashionable. They were popular with college students, young professionals, and homemakers. The company's warm, thick sweaters and indestructible shoes were both handsome and practical. Today, the L. L. Bean store is the main attraction in Freeport. It is so large that it has an indoor trout pond. The post office has even given the mail-order business its own zip code: 04033.

L. L. Bean has done a great deal to promote Maine's image as a rugged, out-of-the-mainstream state. The company operates a series of Outdoor Discovery Schools where students learn to draw maps, shoot with bows and arrows, build campfires, and maintain trail bikes. ■

ing parties. In the fall, the woods are alive with hunters, while winter brings skiers and snowmobilers.

Visitors are drawn to Maine because it seems wild and remote. Yet the influx of tourists has brought shopping malls, fast-food franchises, and traffic jams—all the things the visitors claim they want to escape. In addition, the tourism and timber industries sometimes come into sharp conflict. Hunters and campers from other states are appalled when they find a favorite stretch of forest leveled by clear-cutting, and they often side with the environmentalists. They plead for the preservation of forests and the cleanup of rivers polluted by paper mills. Most Mainers tend to resent this outside interference. They hold that the land is theirs by right, to use as they see fit. It has sustained them for more than 300 years.

Reaching out to the World

Route 1 snakes its way along Maine's eastern edge from Kittery in the south to Madawaska in the far north. For much of the way it is by no means a scenic route. It is lined with strip malls and billboards, and is too far from the shore to offer a view of the sea. But Route 1, like the other roads that crisscross the state, connects Mainers with one another and with the outside world. Today, Maine has 22,577 miles (36,326 km) of roads and highways. Maine is not served by any passenger railroad line. The state has international airports in Portland and Bangor.

Maine's biggest daily newspapers are the *Bangor Daily News* and the *Portland Press-Herald*. WABI, the state's first radio station, began broadcasting from Bangor in 1924. Television came to Maine in 1953 with Bangor's WABI TV. Today, Maine has 107 radio stations and 14 commercial and public television stations.

Standard of Living

In many ways, Mainers have an ideal way of life. In most parts of the state they can breathe clean air, and they seldom have to worry about violent crime. But many of the jobs available in Maine do not pay well. Compared to people in other states, Mainers are relatively poor. In 1997, Maine ranked only thirty-sixth among the states in per capita income. ■

Route 1 through Ellsworth

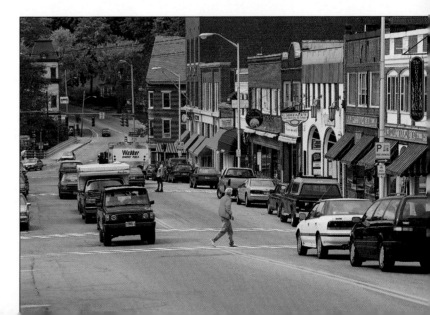

CHAPTER NINE

Down Easters at Home

Much of Maine remains rural.

An old Maine fisherman walked into a bank and handed the teller a check for $98.45. The teller gave him the money. For several minutes the fisher remained at the window, counting his bills and change over and over. At last the teller demanded, "What's the matter? Isn't it all there?" "It is," the fisher grumbled. "Just barely."

This story illustrates the image of the Maine Yankee—flinty, frugal, and never willing to waste words. Few Mainers actually fit this picture, but the notion of the rugged Maine Yankee has certainly helped to shape the character of the state.

Living in the Country

Maine is a state of small cities, smaller towns, and tiny clusters of people who don't live in towns at all. Only 44.6 percent of all Mainers live in urban areas—towns of 2,500 people or more. Demographers, or population experts, consider the remaining 53.4 percent of the population to be rural. By the 1990s, Maine was one of only a handful of states in which the population was still more rural than urban.

Despite these figures, however, few Mainers live on isolated farms in the woods. More than half of the people in the state live within 25 miles (40 km) of the coast. Put another way, half of all

Opposite: Shopping in Freeport

Country Cuisine

Most people think of seafood when they think of Maine recipes. The state is famous for its clambakes and fish fries, and for fresh lobster dripping with melted butter. But Mainers also enjoy a special treat less well known to outsiders—the humble fiddlehead fern. Gathered in the spring, fiddleheads add a delicate, nutty flavor to salads and other dishes. In the 1990s, they saw a surge of popularity, and were carried by many specialty food stores. ■

Mainers live on one-seventh of the state's land. This tendency leaves half of the state largely uninhabited.

In 1990, Maine had a population of 1,233,223, a 9.2 percent population increase since 1980. Maine's population growth is primarily a result of migration from other states. Many people are attracted to Maine because it seems free from such city stresses as noise, pollution, and crime.

Maine stands thirty-eighth in population among the fifty states. Only twelve states have fewer people. Many U.S. cities outrank the entire Pine Tree State when it comes to population. Chicago, for

Boiled Lobster

Maine lobsters are a delicacy, not only in the state, but around the world.

Ingredients:

4 Maine lobsters
2 gallons of saltwater (2 quarts for each lobster)
lobster pot, or other large pot
lemon wedges and melted butter

Directions:

Bring the saltwater to a boil in the lobster pot. Carefully rinse the live lobsters (never cook a dead lobster) in cold water, then drop them into the pot. Allow the water to boil again. Reduce heat to low and cover the pot. If your lobsters weigh 1 pound each, simmer them for 12 minutes (a lobster should be cooked for 12 minutes per pound). Test the lobsters by pulling out one of their antennae. When the antennae come off easily, they are done.

Serve with lemon wedges and melted butter.

Serves 4.

example, has about 2.5 million people, and New York City has more than 7 million.

On average, there are 37 people for every square mile (14 per sq km) of Maine soil. By comparison, Maine's neighbor Massachusetts has 730 people per square mile (282 per sq km). Maine's largest city is Portland, with approximately 64,000 people. Augusta, the state capital, has only 21,000 inhabitants.

Yankees, Etc.

The first Mainers were Native Americans belonging to several Algonquin-speaking tribes. About 6,000 of their descendants live in Maine today. The largest Indian group in the state is the Penobscot, with about 1,200 members. Some 800 people belong to the Passamaquoddy. The Penobscots and Passamaquoddies have about 27,000 acres (11,000 ha) of reservation land. Within both groups, the native languages are gradually disappearing. Only older people still speak them fluently.

The first Europeans to settle on the Maine coast were immigrants from France and England. Later English settlers from Massachusetts migrated north into Maine. The Scotch-Irish comprised another group of early European arrivals. They were the descendants of Scottish people who migrated to Ireland in the 1600s.

The English and Scotch-Irish made up the group often referred to as New England Yankees. Yankees are said to possess a distinctive character. They are sturdy, serious, and fiercely independent. They are careful with their money and cool toward outsiders. Such stereotypes probably have little basis in real-

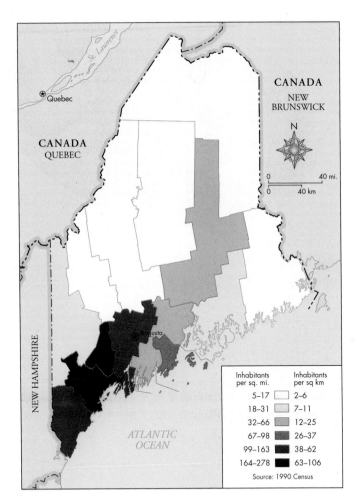

Maine's population density

A French mission on
Mount Desert Island

ity, but one thing does set Maine Yankees apart—the way they speak. Yankees tend to drop their r's. Words such as *border* and *corner* become "bah-dah" and "cah-nah." Yankees are said to have "clipped speech." Because their vowel sounds are short, they seem to speak quickly.

Settlers from France landed in Maine around the same time as the English. Most were driven out after the French and Indian War. However, the French presence remained strong in Quebec and other parts of eastern Canada. French Canadians migrated into Maine as early as the nineteenth century. Some were lured by jobs in Maine's textile mills and other factories. Some bought land and started farms. Today, French is the first language of about 81,000 Mainers.

Population of Maine's Major Cities (1990)

Portland	64,143
Lewiston	39,757
Bangor	33,181
Auburn	24,309
South Portland	23,163
Augusta	21,325

Last of the Abenaki

When the French and Indian Wars ended in 1763, most of the Abenaki Confederacy tribes were driven from Maine into Canada. The Penobscot and the Passamaquoddy are among the few Abenaki tribes who were allowed to remain. Today, they occupy reservations on their traditional land along Maine's upper coast. A representative of the Penobscot and Passamaquoddy people speaks on their behalf in the Maine state legislature, but the Abenaki representatives have no voting privileges. ■

By tradition, Maine Yankees followed a stern Protestant tradition. Many of their ancestors were Puritans from the Massachusetts Bay colony. The Puritans sought to obey the teachings of the Bible as strictly as possible. They looked upon drinking, dancing, and card-playing as the devil's tools. Over the years, Puritan rules eased in Maine, as they did throughout New England. Today, Protestants are still the largest religious group in Maine. Among the numerous Protestant denominations in the state are Congregationalists, Episcopalians, Methodists,

The French Connection

Apart from English, French is the most widely spoken language in Maine today. French-speaking people have lived in Maine since early in the seventeenth century. France once claimed Maine as part of Acadia, a sprawling territory that extended from Quebec to Nova Scotia. During the French and Indian Wars, thousands of Acadians were deported by the English. After a long struggle they made their way to present-day Louisiana. Their descendants are still known as Cajuns, a name derived from the word *Acadian*. ■

Opposite: The Protestant Church has a strong presence in Maine.

Simple Gifts

The Shakers were an austere religious sect that founded colonies in New York and New England late in the eighteenth century. Shakers were not allowed to marry. They lived without adornments or luxuries of any kind, totally dedicated to the worship of God. They were called Shakers because they shook with ecstasy during their church services. Today, Shaker furniture is prized for its exquisite practicality and simplicity.

The last active Shaker community in the United States survives at Sabbathday Lake near New Gloucester, Maine. During the summer, outsiders may visit the 1794 meeting house and several homes and workshops. On display is an assortment of handmade Shaker furniture. Shaker chairs are made so that they can hang from the wall on pegs when the room is being swept. ■

Baptists, and Presbyterians. Maine has about 264,000 Roman Catholics, including most of its French-Canadian citizens. About 8,000 Jews live in the state.

Many ethnic groups are represented in Maine.

Most Mainers are of northern European heritage, but nearly every ethnic group is represented in the state. Maine has about 7,000 Asians, 7,000 Latinos, and 5,000 African-Americans.

The Sorrows of Malaga

In 1794, an African-American fisher named Benjamin Darling settled on Malaga Island off the Maine coast. Other black people joined him, including many runaway slaves. Over the years, members of this tiny black community intermarried with their white neighbors. They lived by fishing and farming.

In 1912, land developers decided they would like to turn Malaga Island into a profitable resort. They pressured the governor of Maine to evict Malaga's long-time residents. The islanders were forced to leave on the grounds that they had never paid for the land. Many children were taken from their parents and made wards of the state. The developers got the land, but Malaga never became popular as a resort. ■

A Little Bit of Difference

The statue of a young Maine girl named Samantha Smith (1972–1985) stands in Augusta. In 1983,

when she was ten years old, Samantha wrote a letter to Yuri Andropov, then premier of the former Soviet Union. At that time there was great tension between the United States and the Soviet Union, which included present-day Russia. In her letter, Samantha Smith pleaded for peace. She wrote, "Congratulations on your new job. I have been worrying about Russia and the United States getting into a nuclear war. Are you going to vote to have a war or not? If you aren't, please tell me how you are going to help to not have a war. This is a question you do not have to answer, but I would like to know why you want to conquer the world, or at least our country. God made the world for us to live together in peace and not to fight."

Premier Andropov was so impressed by Samantha's letter that he invited her to visit his country. Samantha Smith traveled to the Soviet Union as a special ambassador of goodwill. Her message brought a sense of hope to millions of people all over the globe.

Tragically, Samantha Smith and her father were both killed in a plane crash in 1985. Samantha's spirit lives on through a foundation established in her name to promote international understanding. ■

Going to School

Maine is known throughout the nation for its outstanding school system. Elementary-school students often lead the nation with their test scores in math, science, and reading. In 1996, 218,560 students were enrolled in public elementary and secondary schools.

The state of Maine has many excellent colleges and universities. The main campus of the University of Maine is located at Orono. About 31,000 students are enrolled in the University of Maine system. The University of Southern Maine has campuses at Portland and Gorham.

In addition to state-supported universities, Maine has several excellent private colleges. Founded in 1855, Bates College in Lewiston was the first coeducational college on the east coast. The Bates Library contains the papers of Edmund Muskie, one of the school's most famous graduates. Colby College in Waterville

Bates College was founded in 1855.

The Maine Maritime Academy

(founded in 1813) and Bowdoin College in Brunswick (1794) originally accepted only men. Both are now coeducational.

The University of Maine opened in 1862 as a college of agriculture. It was intended to teach the latest, most scientific methods of farming. The state still supports several technical schools that specialize in agriculture, engineering, and electronics. The state-run Maine Maritime Academy is located in Castine.

Alma Mater of Stars

Although it enrolls only 1,400 students, Bowdoin College can count a startling number of famous people among its alumni. Graduates include the poet Henry Wadsworth Longfellow and the novelist Nathaniel Hawthorne. Franklin Pierce, the fourteenth president of the United States, graduated from Bowdoin. So did Robert E. Peary, the Arctic explorer. In 1999, Bowdoin graduate Kenneth I. Chevault was named by the American Express Company to become its chief executive in 2001. He will become one of only two African-American leaders of a Fortune 500 company. ▪

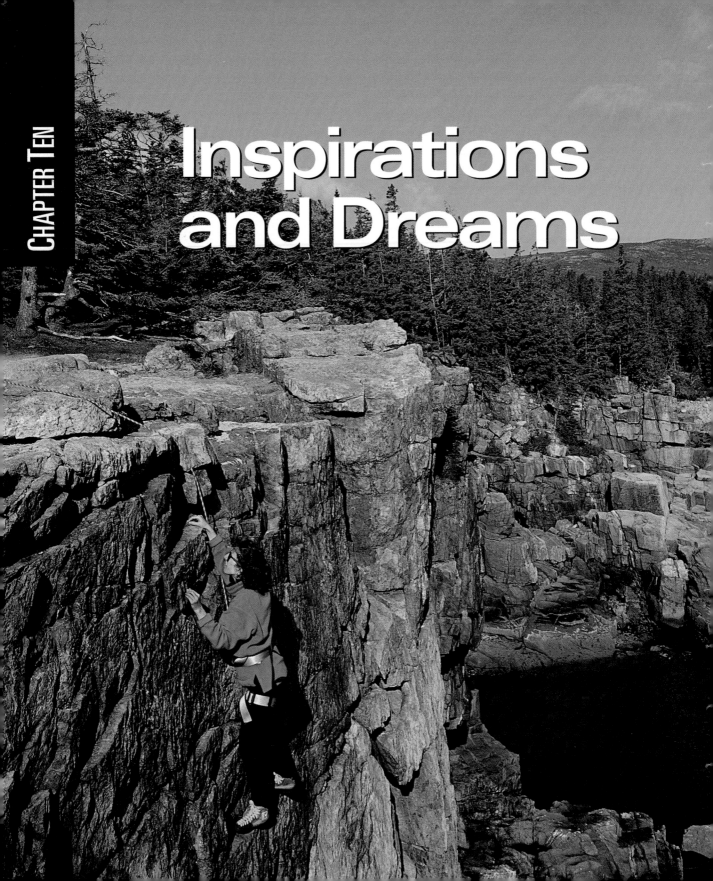

CHAPTER TEN

Inspirations and Dreams

etween the dark and the daylight,
    When the night is beginning to lower,
Comes a pause in the day's occupations,
That is known as the Children's Hour.
    —from "The Children's Hour," by Henry
       Wadsworth Longfellow (1860)

In this poem, loved by generations of Americans, Longfellow recalls some of the happiest moments of his life. Longfellow was born in Portland, where his boyhood home still stands. He is one of a host of poets, novelists, and painters who have drawn inspiration from Maine's scenery and way of life. Athletes as well find Maine a source of inspiration and dreams.

Henry Wadsworth
Longfellow grew up
in Portland.

Pictures in Words

Henry Wadsworth Longfellow (1807–1882) is one of the most popular poets the United States has ever produced. Over the years, millions of schoolchildren have memorized such poems as "Paul Revere's Ride," which begins with the famous lines: "Listen my children, and you shall hear/ Of the midnight ride of Paul Revere." Longfellow grew up in Portland and attended Bowdoin College in Brunswick. After studying in Europe for four years, he returned to Bowdoin as a professor of modern languages. Longfellow eventually moved to Massachusetts, but many of his poems reflect his roots in Maine. Among them is "Evangeline," the story of the Acadians and their deportation to Louisiana.

Opposite: Climbing at
Acadia National Park

Sarah Orne Jewett at home in Maine

Sarah Orne Jewett (1849–1909) spent most of her life in the coastal town of South Berwick. Her father was a doctor, and as a child she often went with him when he visited his patients. She came to know fishers, herb gatherers, farmers, midwives, and a host of other local characters. Jewett's writing captures the speech patterns and daily lives of these ordinary people. Her 1884 novel *A Country Doctor* is a loving portrait of her father. Her best-known work, *The Country of the Pointed Firs* (1896) describes the elderly residents of a small Maine town.

In 1912, a twenty-year-old woman won national attention when she published a long poem called "Renascence." The young poet was Edna St. Vincent Millay (1892–1950) of Rockland, Maine. Millay's sudden fame earned her a scholarship to Vassar College in Poughkeepsie, New York. Her work was immensely popular during the 1920s, and she won the Pulitzer Prize for Poetry in 1923.

Remembering South Berwick

"I am proud to have been made of Berwick dust, and a little of it is apt to fly in my eyes," wrote Sarah Orne Jewett. "It makes them blur whenever I tell the stories of bravery, of fine ambition, of the love of friend for friend and the kindness of neighbor to neighbor in this beloved town." One of Jewett's cherished causes was the preservation of Hamilton House, a beautiful mansion built in South Berwick in 1787. Thanks to Jewett's efforts, Hamilton House is now one of Maine's most treasured historic homes. ∎

Though she spent most of her time in New York and Europe, Millay returned to Maine to pass many happy summers on Ragged Island near Brunswick.

Kenneth Roberts (1885–1957) was the author of a series of vivid historical novels set during the colonial era and around the time of the American Revolution. His most famous book, *Northwest Passage*, was made into a popular movie. Many of Roberts's tales took place in the fictional village of Arundel on the Maine coast. Eventually, the actual town of North Kennebunk changed its name to Arundel in honor of Roberts's novels.

Since it first appeared in 1952, millions of children have delighted in E. B. White's

Edna St. Vincent Millay in 1934

"Renascence"

Edna St. Vincent Millay's poem "Renascence" recounts a journey from depression to spiritual awakening. The word *renascence* means "rebirth." Many of the images in the poem were inspired by the coast around Rockland. The poem begins with the famous lines:

> *All I could see from where I stood*
> *Was three long mountains and a wood;*
> *I turned and looked another way,*
> *And saw three islands in a bay.*
> *So with my eyes I traced the line*
> *Of the horizon, thin and fine,*
> *Straight around till I was come*
> *Back to where I'd started from.* ■

E. B. White at work at *The New Yorker*

charming novel *Charlotte's Web*. The book tells the story of a pig named Wilbur and his friend Charlotte, a clever spider who saves him from being turned into bacon. Elwyn Brooks (E. B.) White (1899–1985) spent many summers in North Brooklin on Penobscot Bay. He wrote witty, thoughtful essays for *The New Yorker* and other literary magazines. But he is best loved for his children's classics *Stuart Little* (1945) and *Charlotte's Web* (1952).

The master of horror, Stephen King, was born in Portland in 1947. He later made his home in Bangor. King's chilling novels test ordinary people against the forces of evil. Many of King's books, including *Salem's Lot* (1975) and *Bag of Bones* (1998), take place in King's native state. Many of King's novels have been turned into movies.

Pictures to Gaze Upon

Thomas Cole (1801–1848) is remembered chiefly as a founder of the Hudson River School of American art. His paintings of the bluffs along the Hudson shimmer with light. But Cole did not limit himself to the land-scapes of upstate New York. He took long journeys on foot, exploring many parts of New England. A few years before his death Cole found himself on Mount Desert Island off the coast of Maine. He was entranced by the island's rugged beauty, and returned as often as he could.

Cole's discovery led many other artists to Maine. The most famous among them was Winslow Homer (1836–1910). Homer spent the last twenty years of his life at Prout's Neck (now part of

Stephen King lives in Bangor and sets many of his novels in Maine.

The Basketmaker's Art

During the 1880s and 1890s, Native American women used to visit rusticator cottages, selling handmade baskets from door to door. By the early 1990s, traditional basketmaking was almost a lost art. Only a few dozen Indian women in north-eastern Maine remembered the weaving methods they had learned from their mothers and grandmothers. But today crafts-people in Maine are taking a renewed interest in basketry, rescuing this dying art from oblivion.

Indian baskets are sturdy and lightweight. They are made of strips of birch or ash bark known as splints, and lined with a reed called sweetgrass. Some-times the baskets are tinted with natural dyes made from berries and roots. Indian men once wove large, rough baskets used by farmers to hold potatoes. Many fine examples of Indian baskets are on display at the Abbe Museum on Mount Desert Island. ■

Winslow Homer

Portland). His watercolors and oil paintings depict people involved with the sea. *The Lifeline* shows a woman being rescued from a shipwreck. In *Driftwood* a fisher struggles to haul a heavy log ashore.

Like Winslow Homer, Rockwell Kent (1882–1971) often painted seascapes and ships. Kent began his professional career as an architect, but he soon grew restless and turned to a life of adventure. He explored such far-flung places as Alaska, Newfoundland, and Tierra del Fuego at the southern tip of South America. He also worked as a ship's carpenter and a lobsterman on the Maine coast. Many of his paintings reflect his love for Maine's rocky islands and misty harbors. Kent was one of several painters who often gathered at the lighthouse on Monhegan Island to discuss their work.

Andrew Wyeth (1917–), probably the most popular U.S. painter of the late twentieth century, does much of his best work at

Clay, Cloth, and Yarn

Every summer, potters, weavers, and other craftspeople flock to the Haystack Mountain School of Crafts on Deer Isle near Castine. The school perches on a steep hill overlooking Jericho Bay. Students work in sunlit studios connected by plank walkways. Many of their works are for sale at the school's gallery. ■

An Artist's Delight

Every year, artists and photographers, both amateur and professional, explore Maine's back roads in search of covered bridges. These structures, with their rustic wooden roofs, are a favorite subject for pictures. Most covered bridges were built in the nineteenth and early twentieth centuries. The roofs protected the timbers of the bridge from damage because of ice and snow. At one time Maine had 120 covered bridges, but today only 9 survive.

One of the best-known covered bridges in Maine is the Sunday River Bridge in Newry near North Bethel. It is sometimes called the Artists Bridge because it has been painted so often. Babb's Bridge crosses the Presumpscot River north of Gorham. Fire destroyed Babb's Bridge in 1973, but it has been faithfully reconstructed. The oldest covered bridge in Maine is the Hemlock Bridge over the Saco River near East Fryeburg, built in 1857. ■

The Lily of the North

Born in Farmington, Maine, Lillian Nordica (1859–1914) rose to prominence as one of the leading opera singers of her time. Though she left the Pine Tree State when she was six years old, she always regarded herself as a Mainer. Her fans affectionately nicknamed her "The Lily of the North." Nordica's birthplace is preserved as a historic house in Farmington. Memorabilia from her career are on display, including some of the elaborate costumes she wore in U.S. and European productions. ■

his summer cottage in Cushing, Maine. Wyeth is fascinated by old houses, stone walls, and gnarled old trees. Maine furnishes him with plenty of material.

When she was five years old, Louise Nevelson (1900–1988) moved with her family from Kiev in Russia to Rockland on Maine's Penobscot Bay. In her late teens, Nevelson went to New York City, where she studied painting and sculpture at the Art Students League. She is best known for her large, abstract wood sculptures, usually painted black, white, or gold. Because her works are composed of many parts fitted together, Nevelson called them "assemblages."

Paintings and sculptures by many of the state's most accomplished artists are on view in Maine's galleries and museums. Museums that specialize in Maine artists include the Portland Museum of Art, Ogunquit Museum of American Art, Bowdoin Museum of Art in Brunswick, and the Farnsworth Museum in Rockland. The Farnsworth Museum was founded and supported by sculptor Louise Nevelson.

Mainers on the Move

Because Maine has no major-league sports teams, most Mainers follow teams from Boston. During the football season they root for the New England Patriots. In basketball they favor the Boston Celtics, in baseball they cheer for the Boston Red Sox. Mainers are also avid hockey enthusiasts. The state's strong minor-league hockey team, the Portland Pirates, draws capacity crowds at Cumberland County Civic Center in Portland.

The sculpture garden at the Ogunquit Museum of American Art

Ships Ahoy!

Every year on a morning in July, crowds gather at Maine's Boothbay Harbor to watch the annual Boothbay Windjammer Festival. The graceful sailing craft are a breathtaking sight as they take to the sea. Like Maine sailors of old, the crews who sail these modern ships rely on a knowledge of currents and winds. ■

The Perfect Wave

Most people think that surfing is a sport only for warm southern seas. But some hardy surfers find happiness in the crashing breakers off the coast of Maine. The warming currents of the Gulf Stream do not reach this far north, and the sea is icy cold, even in early summer. Maine surfers tackle the waves encased in rubber wet suits, but they insist that the waves are glorious. ■

In the late 1990s, college women's basketball soared to spectacular heights in Maine. Its sudden rise was due largely to the extraordinary talent of Cindy Blodgett, a forward with the University of Maine Black Bears. When she was only a third-grader in the town of Fairfield, a local coach spotted Blodgett's talent and arranged for her to join the town's high school team. After graduating from the university in 1998, Cindy Blodgett planned to train for the U.S. Olympic team.

What Maine lacks in professional teams it makes up for in indi-
vidual sports. Mainers and visitors alike throw themselves into a
host of outdoor activities. They hike Maine's stretch of the
Appalachian Trail, tackle Mount Katahdin, and swim, sail, and
canoe. In the winter, they put on ice skates and glide across frozen
lakes, or zoom down hillsides on skis. The sea and the forest shape
the ways people play and relax in Maine, just as they have shaped
the state's character throughout its long history.

**Taking a break to
enjoy the view**

Timeline

United States History

Maine State History

ca. 900   Vikings land along coast of Maine.

ca. 1500   English explorer John Cabot sails along Maine coast.

1524   Giovanni da Verrazano explores Maine's coastline.

1604   Captain John Smith sails to Casco Bay and tries to count the islands. French explorer Samuel de Champlain settles on the St. Croix River and establishes a colony.

The first permanent English settlement is established in North America at Jamestown. **1607**

1607   English colonists establish Popham Plantation on the Kennebec River. They leave it the following year because of the harsh winter and American Indian attacks.

Pilgrims found Plymouth Colony, the second permanent English settlement. **1620**

1622   King Charles I divides land between two land owners, John Mason and Ferdinando Gorges. Gorges's share becomes the province of Maine.

1636   Maine's first government is established.

1677   Gorges's heirs sell Maine to Massachusetts.

1775   The first naval battle of Revolutionary War is fought in Maine's Machias Bay, when colonists capture the British ship *Margaretta*.

America declares its independence from Britain. **1776**

Treaty of Paris officially ends the Revolutionary War in America. **1783**

U.S. Constitution is written. **1787**

Louisiana Purchase almost doubles the size of the United States. **1803**

United States History

U.S. and Britain 1812–15
fight the War of 1812.

The North and South fight 1861–65
each other in the American Civil War.

The United States is 1917–18
involved in World War I.

The stock market crashes, plunging 1929
the United States into the
Great Depression.

The United States fights in 1941–45
World War II.

The United States becomes a 1945
charter member of the
United Nations.

The United States fights 1951–53
in the Korean War.

The U.S. Congress enacts a series of 1964
groundbreaking civil rights laws.

The United States 1964–73
engages in the Vietnam War.

The United States and other 1991
nations fight the brief Persian
Gulf War against Iraq.

Maine State History

1820 Maine becomes the twenty-third state on March 15.

1842 The Aroostook War is settled under the Webster-Ashburton Treaty, under which Maine gives up 5,500 square miles (14,245 sq km) of land to Canada.

1851 Maine is the first state to outlaw manufacture and sale of alcohol.

1909 Shipbuilders at the Bath Ironworks begin building the ship *Wyoming*, the largest ship ever built in the United States.

1934 Maine repeals its prohibition law.

1980 Penobscot and Passamaquoddy Indians win $81.5 million in a lawsuit filed to reclaim 12.5 million acres (5.1 million ha) of land taken from them during the eighteenth century.

Fast Facts

A moose

Statehood date	March 15, 1820, the 23rd state
Origin of state name	Probably referring to the mainland as distinct from the many coastal islands
State capital	Augusta
State nicknames	Pine Tree State, Vacationland
State motto	*Dirigo* (I direct or I lead)
State bird	Black-capped chickadee
State flower	White pine cone and tassel
State animal	Moose
State fish	Landlocked salmon
State insect	Honeybee
State mineral	Tourmaline
State song	"State of Maine Song"
State fair	Timonium, late August–early September
Total area; rank	33,741 sq. mi. (87,389 sq km); 39th
Land; rank	30,865 sq. mi. (79,940 sq km); 39th
Water; rank	2,878 sq. mi. (7,448 sq km); 13th
***Inland water;* rank**	2,263 sq. mi. (5,861 sq km); 9th
***Coastal water;* rank**	613 sq. mi. (1,588 sq km); 9th

A honeybee

Portland

Some of Maine's students

Geographic center	Piscataquis, north of Dover
Latitude and longitude	Maine is located approximately between 43° 04′ and 47° 28′ N and 65° 57′ and 71° 07′ W
Highest point	Mount Katahdin, 5,268 feet (1,606 m)
Lowest point	Sea level along the coast
Largest city	Portland
Number of counties	16
Population; rank	1,233,223 (1990 census); 38th
Density	37 persons per sq. mi. (14 per sq km)
Population distribution	45% urban, 55% rural

Ethnic distribution (total does not equal 100%)		
White		98.41%
Hispanic		0.56%
Native American		0.49%
African-American		0.42%
Asian and Pacific Islanders		0.54%
Other		0.14%

Record high temperature	105°F (41°C) at North Bridgton on July 10, 1911
Record low temperature	−48°F (−44°C) at Van Buren on January 19, 1925
Average July temperature	67°F (19°C)
Average January temperature	15°F (−9°C)
Average annual precipitation	41 inches (104 cm)

The cliffs of Acadia
National Park

Appalachian National
Scenic Trail

Natural Areas and Historic Sites

National Park

Acadia National Park covers approximately 42,000 acres (17,000 ha) including most of Mount Desert Island off the coast of Maine. A small part of the park is on Schoodic Peninsula and another part is on Isle au Haut.

National Scenic Trail

Appalachian National Scenic Trail follows the Appalachian Mountains from Maine to Georgia, a total of 2,158 miles (3,473 km).

International Historic Site

Saint Croix Island International Historic Site commemorates the French attempt to settle the island in 1604.

National Forests

White Mountain National Forest is the largest alpine area east of the Rockies and south of Canada. A part of this forest lies in Maine.

State Parks

Maine maintains a system of thirty state parks that provide year-round activities for visitors.

Grafton Notch State Park has interesting roadside hikes and vistas, notably Screw Auger Falls Gorge.

Baxter State Park, in northern Maine, is the state's largest park at 200,000 acres (80,000 ha). Former governor Percival P. Baxter donated the land to be maintained as a wilderness area and wildlife sanctuary. The state's highest point, Baxter Peak, is in the southern section of the park.

Stevens Hall

Sports Teams

NCAA Teams (Division 1)

University of Maine Black Bears

Cultural Institutions

Libraries

Maine has 225 libraries. Outstanding collections are housed at the *University of Maine*, the *Maine Historical Society* (Portland), and the *Maine State Library* (Augusta).

Museums

Portland Museum of Art has a fine collection of eighteenth- and nineteenth-century American artists.

Bowdoin College Museum of Art holds important works by American artists.

The Peary-MacMillan Art Museum highlights polar artifacts and exploration materials.

Robert Abbe Museum of Stone Age Antiquities maintains an extensive Native American collection.

Maine Historical Society (Portland) houses Native American artifacts, as does the *State Museum* (Augusta).

Performing Arts

Maine has two major symphony orchestras.

Universities and Colleges

In the mid-1990s, Maine had fourteen public and seventeen private institutions of higher learning.

Bates College

Annual Events

January–June

Winter activities in Bethel, Carrabassett Valley, Greenville, Jackman, Kingfield, Rangeley, and other places (January–February)

International skiing events at Sugarloaf/Carrabassett (January–April)

World Mogul Invitational at Newry (March)

Maine Maple Sunday is celebrated statewide (March)

Acadian Festival at Madawaska (June)

July–December

Clam Festival in Yarmouth (July)

Belfast Bay Festival in Belfast (July)

Crown of Maine Balloon Festival at Caribou (July)

Windjammer Days at Boothbay Harbor (July)

Great Kennebec Whatever Festival at Augusta (July)

Potato Blossom Festival at Fort Fairfield (July)

World's Fastest Lobster Boat Races at Jonesport (July)

Lobster Festival at Rockland (August)

Blueberry Festival in Union (August)

Northern Maine Fair at Presque Isle (August)

Maine Festival of the Arts in Portland (August)

Retired Skippers Race in Castine (August)

Common Ground Country Fair in Unity (September)

Fairs in Bangor, Cumberland Center, Farmington, Fryeburg, Presque Isle, Skowhegan, Topsham, Union, and Windsor (various times during the summer and in early autumn)

Boothbay Harbor

Famous People

Henry Wadsworth Longfellow

Edna St. Vincent Millay

Cyrus H. K. Curtis (1850–1933)	Publisher
Dorothea Lynde Dix (1802–1887)	Educator and social reformer
Melville Weston Fuller (1833–1910)	U.S. chief justice
Hannibal Hamlin (1809–1891)	U.S. vice president
Sarah Orne Jewett (1849–1909)	Author
Stephen King (1947–)	Author
Henry Wadsworth Longfellow (1807–1882)	Poet
Hiram Stevens Maxim (1840–1916)	Inventor
Edna St. Vincent Millay (1892–1950)	Poet
Edmund Muskie (1914–1996)	U.S. senator
Sir William Phips (1651–1695)	Colonial governor
Kenneth Lewis Roberts (1885–1957)	Author
Edward Arlington Robinson (1869–1935)	Poet
Nelson Aldrich Rockefeller (1908–1979)	Public official, U.S. vice president
Margaret Chase Smith (1897–1995)	U.S. congresswoman

To Find Out More

History

- Engfer, LeeAnne. *Maine.* Minneapolis: Lerner, 1991.
- Fendler, Don. *Lost on a Mountain in Maine: A Brave Boy's True Story of His Nine-Day Adventure Alone in the Mount Katahdin Wilderness.* Brookfield, Conn.: Beech Tree Books, 1992.
- Fradin, Dennis Brindell. *Maine.* Chicago: Childrens Press, 1994.
- Kress, Stephen W., and Pete Salmansohn. *Project Puffin: How We Brought Puffins Back to Egg Rock.* Gardiner, Me.: Tilbury House Publishers, 1997.
- Thompson, Kathleen. *Maine.* Austin, Tex.: Raintree/Steck Vaughn, 1996.

Fiction

- MacLachlan, Patricia. *Skylark.* New York: HarperCollins, 1994.
- Voigt, Cynthia. *Tree by Leaf.* New York: Atheneum, 1998.

Biographies

- Anderson, Peter. *Henry David Thoreau: American Naturalist.* New York: Franklin Watts, 1995.
- Beneduce, Ann K. *A Weekend with Winslow Homer.* Manhasett, N.Y.: Rizzoli, 1993.
- Jacobs, William Jay. *Champlain: A Life of Courage.* New York: Franklin Watts, 1994.
- Kent, Zachary. *George Bush.* Chicago: Childrens Press, 1989.

Websites

■ **Maine Map of WWW Resources**
http://www.destek.net/Maps/ME.html
Links to many websites related to Maine

■ **Maine State Government**
http://www.state.me.us
The official website for the state of Maine

Addresses

■ **Maine Publicity Bureau**
P.O. Box 2300
Hallowell, ME 04347
For information on travel and tourism in Maine, as well as Maine's history

■ **Maine Department of Economic and Community Development**
State House Station 59
Augusta, ME 04333
For information on Maine's economy and government

Index

Page numbers in *italics* indicate illustrations.

Meet the Author

Deborah Kent grew up in Little Falls, New Jersey. She received a bachelor's degree in English from Oberlin College and a master's degree from Smith College School for Social Work. After working for four years at the University Settlement House in New York City, she decided to pursue her dream of becoming a writer. She left New York for San Miguel de Allende, Mexico, a town with a thriving community of writers and artists. In San Miguel, she wrote her first book, a young-adult novel called *Belonging*.

Kent is the author of fifteen novels for young adults, as well as many nonfiction books for middle-grade readers. Her nonfiction titles include several books in the America the Beautiful series. Kent lives in Chicago with her husband, children's-book author R. Conrad Stein, and their daughter Janna.

When Kent was twelve, she and her parents spent a week in northern Maine. They stayed at a fishing camp in an area so

remote that it could not be reached by car. They had to fly in on a small plane that landed on the lake. Kent has never forgotten the old-timer who told stories by the fire in the evenings, or the wild laughter of the loons as they splashed and dove at dusk. One day she went on a long hike with a guide. At the top of a hill, the guide pointed to the north, south, east, and west, and told her that unbroken forest stretched for more than fifty miles in every direction. Coming from crowded New Jersey, she was thrilled by the thought of so much wilderness.

Ever since that first visit, Kent has had a special fondness for the state of Maine. Maine has seen enormous changes over the years, but Kent still finds it full of wonderful surprises.

Photo Credits

Photographs ©:

Art Resource, NY: 18 (Giraudon)
Collections of Maine Historical Society: 41 (Douglas), 43, 44, 45
Corbis-Bettmann: 69, 93, 119, 120, 135 bottom (UPI), 33 (Baldwin H. Ward), 16, 27, 37, 117, 118, 122, 124, 135 top
David J. Forbert: 9
Dean Abramson: 6 top middle, 70, 76, 80, 95, 104, 114, 131 top, 133 bottom
Envision: 107 (Henry T. Kaiser)
Gene Ahrens: 7 top center, 11, 12, 51, 52, 68, 84, 111, 132 top
H. Armstrong Roberts, Inc.: 123 (T. Algire), 8 (F. Sieb)
International Stock Photo: 2 (Michael Von Ruber)
Monkmeyer Press: 28 (Goodwin), 53 (Kagan)
National Geographic Image Collection: 54 (Raymond)
New England Stock Photo: 50, 98, 105, 126, 134 (Kip Brundasp), 55, 116, 132 bottom (Peter Cole), 112, 131 bottom (Jeff Greenberg), 47, 66, 85, 86, 103, 115 (Jim Schwabel), 6 top left, 48, 97, 101 (Kevin Shields), 125, 127
North Wind Picture Archives: 13, 75

(N. Carter), 6 bottom, 14, 17, 19, 21, 25, 26, 29, 31, 32, 34, 35, 36, 38, 39, 42, 63, 73, 109, 113
Photo Researchers: 90 bottom right (Roberto De Gugliemo/SPL), 90 bottom left, 130 bottom (E. R. Degginger), 90 top, 130 top (Michael P. Gadomski), 22 (Gale Koschmann Belinky), 58 bottom (Stephen J. Kraseman), 106 (M. dos Passos), 7 bottom, 58 top (Farrell Grehan)
Stanley Museum, Kingfield, Maine: 100
Stock Montage, Inc.: 92
Superstock, Inc.: 49 top
The Image Works: 67 (Townsend P. Dickinson)
Tony Stone Images: 94 (Sara Gray), back cover (David Muench), 7 top left, 40 (Phil Schermeister)
University of Maine Public Affairs: 79, 133 top
Visuals Unlimited: 6 top right, 99 (Jeff Greenberg), 59 (Gary Meszaros)
Voscar: cover, 7 top right, 24, 30, 49 bottom, 57, 60, 61, 64, 72, 77, 82, 89, 102, 121
Maps by XNR Productions, Inc.